The Printer I

Or, How Benjamin Franklin Ma[de]
Example for Youth.

William Makepeace Thayer

Alpha Editions

This edition published in 2024

ISBN 9789362511164

Design and Setting By
Alpha Editions
www.alphaedis.com
Email - info@alphaedis.com

As per information held with us this book is in Public Domain.
This book is a reproduction of an important historical work.
Alpha Editions uses the best technology to reproduce historical work
in the same manner it was first published to preserve its original nature.
Any marks or number seen are left intentionally to preserve.

Contents

PREFACE. - 2 -
CHAPTER I. - 3 -
CHAPTER II. - 8 -
CHAPTER III. - 14 -
CHAPTER IV. - 19 -
CHAPTER V. - 28 -
CHAPTER VI. - 34 -
CHAPTER VII. - 39 -
CHAPTER VIII. - 45 -
CHAPTER IX. - 50 -
CHAPTER X. - 55 -
CHAPTER XI. - 61 -
CHAPTER XII. - 67 -
CHAPTER XIII. - 73 -
CHAPTER XIV. - 77 -
CHAPTER XV. - 81 -
CHAPTER XVI. - 87 -
CHAPTER XVII. - 100 -
CHAPTER XVIII. - 105 -
CHAPTER XIX. - 113 -
CHAPTER XX. - 117 -
CHAPTER XXI. - 122 -
CHAPTER XXII. - 131 -
CHAPTER XXIII. - 136 -

CHAPTER XXIV.	- 145 -
CHAPTER XXV.	- 151 -

"How much did you give for your whistle!"—See page 4.

PREFACE.

THIS book is designed to illustrate the familiar maxim, that "THE BOY IS FATHER TO THE MAN." The early life of Franklin is sketched from his childhood to the time he was established in business, thus showing what he was in boyhood and youth; and the achievements of his manhood are summed up in a closing chapter, to substantiate the truth of the above proverb.

The author believes that the lives of distinguished men may be incorporated into a story, uniting narrative and dialogue so as to be more attractive to the young. John Bunyan was the first to adopt this style, and his inimitable Pilgrim's Progress charms the young reader, not only by its graphic imagery, but also by its alternation of narrative and dialogue. Since his day, others have adopted a similar style, particularly in works of fiction, with success. Why may not truth appear in such a dress as successfully as fiction? Why may not *actual* lives be presented in this manner as vividly as *imaginary* ones? The young mind will seize upon a truth or fact that is conveyed in a story, when it will remain wholly indifferent to it as it appears in a simple statement. So the life of an eminent man may engage the attention of this class, if he is made to speak and act for himself, when they would not be interested in it, if it were presented to them in a plain summary of facts.

In this volume, the actual, early life of Franklin is wrought into a story. The imagination has done no more than weave the facts of his boyhood and youth into a "tale of real life." It makes Benjamin and his associates speak and do what biographers say they spoke and did. It simply paints the scenes and acts of which other writers have *told*.

A conspicuous place is given in the work to the maxims of Franklin, for the purpose of conveying important lessons in regard to the formation of character, and thus stimulating the young in the path of well-doing. Whole volumes of meaning are condensed into many of his wise and pithy sayings.

W. M. T.

CHAPTER I.

THE WHISTLE.

IT was a bright, welcome holiday to little Benjamin Franklin, when his kind parents put some coppers into his pocket, to spend as he saw fit. Possibly it was the first time he was ever permitted to go out alone into the streets of Boston with money to spend for his own pleasure; for he was now but seven years old.

"Can I have more coppers when these are gone?" he inquired.

"No," replied his mother, "you have quite as many now as will be for your welfare, I think. You must be a good boy, and keep out of mischief."

"What are you going to buy?" asked an older brother; and without waiting for a reply, he answered the question himself, by saying, "Candy, of course."

"Lay out your money wisely," added his mother; "I shall want to see how much wisdom you display in your purchases. Remember 'all is not gold that glitters.'"

His mother had scarcely ceased speaking, when Benjamin bounded out of the house, eager to enjoy the anticipated pleasures of the day. Like other boys, on such occasions, his head was filled with bewitching fancies, and he evidently expected such a day of joy as he never had before. First in his thoughts stood the toy-shop, into the windows of which he had often looked wistfully, although it was a small affair compared with the Boston toy-shops of the present day. Every article in it could have been examined in one or two hours, while now it would take as many days to view all the articles in one of these curiosity-shops. It is almost wonderful, and even fabulous, this multiplication of playthings for the children. There seems to be no end to them, and many a girl and boy have been put to their "wits' end" to know what to choose out of the thousands of articles arranged on the shelves.

Benjamin had not proceeded far before he met a boy blowing away upon, a new-bought whistle, as if its music were sweeter than the voice of lark or nightingale. He could scarcely help envying him the happiness of owning so valuable a treasure. He stopped and looked at him with an expression of delight, and they exchanged glances that showed a genuine sympathy springing up between them. At once he resolved to possess a similar musical instrument, as I suppose it may be called; and away he hastened to the toy-shop, knowing that it must have been purchased there.

"Any whistles?" he inquired.

"Plenty of them," answered the proprietor, with a smile, as he brought forth a number, to the amazement of his little customer.

"I will give you all the money I have for one," said Benjamin, without waiting to inquire the price, so enthusiastic was he to become the possessor of such a prize.

"Ah! all you have?" responded the merchant. "Perhaps you have not so much as I ask for them. You see these are very nice whistles."

"I know it," added Benjamin, "and I will give you all the money I have for one," still more afraid that he should not be able to obtain one.

"How much money have you?"

Benjamin told him honestly just how much he had, and the merchant agreed to give him a whistle in exchange for it.

Never was a child more delighted than he, when the bargain was made. He tried every whistle, that he might select the one having the most music in it; and when his choice was settled, he turned his steps towards home. He thought no more of other sights and scenes, and cared not for sweetmeats and knick-knacks, now that he owned this wonderful thing. He reached home and hurried into the house, blowing his whistle lustily as he went, as if he expected to astonish the whole race of Franklins by the shrillness, if not by the sweetness, of his music.

"What have you there, Benjamin?" inquired his mother.

"A whistle," he answered, hardly stopping his blowing long enough to give a reverent reply.

"You got back quick, it seems to me," she continued. "Have you seen all that is to be seen?"

"All I want to see," he answered; which was very true. He was so completely carried away with his whistle that he had lost all his interest in everything else belonging to the holiday. His cup of delight was running over now that he could march about the house with musical sounds of his own making.

"How much did you give for your whistle?" asked one of his cousins, who was present.

"All the money I had," he replied.

"What!" exclaimed his brother, "did you give all your money for that little concern?"

"Yes, every cent of it."

"You are not half so bright as I thought you were," continued his brother. "It is four times as much as the whistle is worth."

"You should have asked the price of it, in the first place," said his mother. "Some men will take all the money they can get for an article. Perhaps he did not ask so much as you gave for it."

"If you had given a reasonable price for it," said his brother, "you might have had enough left to have bought a pocketful of good things."

"Yes," added his cousin, "peppermints, candy, cakes, and more perhaps; but it is the first time he ever went a shopping on a holiday."

"I must confess you are a smart fellow, Ben" (as he was familiarly called by the boys), "to be taken in like that," continued his brother, rather deridingly. "All your money for that worthless thing, that is enough to make us crazy! You ought to have known better. Suppose you had had twice as much money, you would have given it all for the whistle, I suppose, if this is the way you trade."

"Perhaps he would have bought two or three of them in that case," said his cousin, at the same time looking very much as if he intended to make sport of the young whistler.

By this time Benjamin, who had said nothing in reply to their taunts and reproofs, was running over with feeling, and he could hold in no longer. He burst into tears, and made even more noise by crying than he had done with his whistle. Both their ridicule and the thought of having paid so much more than he ought for the article, overcame him, and he found relief in tears. His mother came to the rescue, by saying—

"Never mind, Benjamin, you will understand better next time. We must all live and learn. Perhaps you did about as well as most boys of your age would."

"I think so, too," said his cousin; "but we wanted to have a little sport, seeing it is a holiday. So wipe up, 'Ben,' and we will have a good time yet."

On the whole, it was really a benefit that Benjamin paid too much for his whistle. For he learned a lesson thereby which he never forgot. It destroyed his happiness on that holiday, but it saved him from much unhappiness in years to come. More than sixty years afterwards, when he was in France, he wrote to a friend, rehearsing this incident of his childhood, and said—

"This, however, was afterwards of use to me, the impression continuing on my mind; so that often, when I was tempted to buy some unnecessary thing, I said to myself, *Don't give too much for the whistle*; and I saved my money.

"As I grew up, came into the world, and observed the actions of men, I thought I met with many, very many who *gave too much for the whistle*.

"When I saw one too ambitious of court favour, sacrificing his time in attendance on levées, his repose, his liberty, his virtue, and, perhaps, his friends, to attain it, I have said to myself, *This man gives too much for his whistle*.

"When I saw another fond of popularity, constantly employing himself in political bustles, neglecting his own affairs, and ruining them by that neglect, *He pays, indeed*, said I, *too much for his whistle*.

"If I see one fond of appearance, or fine clothes, fine houses, fine furniture, fine equipages, all above his fortune, for which he contracts debts, and ends his career in a prison, *Alas!* say I, *he has paid dear, very dear for his whistle*.

"When I see a beautiful, sweet-tempered girl married to an ill-natured brute of a husband, *What a pity*, say I, *that she should pay so much for a whistle!*

"In short, I conceive that great part of the miseries of mankind are brought upon them by the false estimates they have made of the value of things, and by their *giving too much for their whistle*."

Thus Benjamin made a good use of one of the foolish acts of his boyhood, which tells well for both his head and heart. Many boys are far less wise, and do the same foolish thing over and over again. They never learn wisdom from the past. Poor, simple, pitiable class of boys!

Let the reader prove himself another Benjamin Franklin in this respect. Remember that there is more than one way *to pay too dear for a whistle*, and he is wisest who tries to discover them all.

When a boy equivocates, or deceives, to conceal some act of disobedience from his parents or teachers, and thereby lays the foundations for habitual untruthfulness, he pays too dear for the whistle; and he will learn the truth of it when he becomes older, and cannot command the confidence of his friends and neighbours, but is branded by them as an unreliable, dishonest man.

In like manner, the boy who thinks it is manly to smoke, and fill the wine-cup, will find that he has a very expensive whistle, when he becomes "hail fellow well met" among a miserable class of young men, and is despised and discarded by the virtuous and good.

So, in general, the young person who is fascinated by worldly pleasure, and supposes that wealth and honour are real apples of gold to the possessor, thinking less of goodness and a life of piety than he does of mere show and worldliness, will find that he has been playing with a costly whistle, when age and his last sickness comes, and death confronts him with its stern realities.

CHAPTER II.

AT SCHOOL.

"WELL, Benjamin," said his father, laying down his violin, upon which he was wont to play in the evening, for his own and children's amusement, "how should you like to go to school and qualify yourself to be a minister? You are as fond of your books as James is of printing, or John of making candles!"

"I should like to go to school well enough," replied Benjamin, after some hesitation; "but I don't know about the rest of it."

"You are old enough now," continued his father, "to think about a trade or profession. Your elder brothers have their trades, and, perhaps, you ought to give your service to the Church. You like to study, do you not?"

"Yes, sir; the best of anything I do." A very correct answer, since he began to read so young, that he could not remember the time when he could not read his Bible.

"It will cost a good deal to keep you at school and educate you, and perhaps I shall not be able to do it with so large a family to support. I have to be very industrious now to make my ends meet. But if you are diligent to improve your time, and lend a helping hand at home, out of school hours, I may be able to do it."

"When shall I begin, if you decide to let me go?"

"Immediately. It is a long process to become qualified for the ministry, and the sooner you begin the better."

"Uncle Benjamin," as he was called in the family, a brother of our little hero's father, sat listening to the conversation, and, at this point, remarked, "Yes, Benjamin, it is the best thing you can do. I am sure you can make very rapid progress at school; and there ought to be one preacher in the family, I think."

"So many people have told me," added his father. "Dr. Willard (his pastor) said as much to me not long ago, and I am fully persuaded to make the trial."

"It won't be a severe trial, either," said Uncle Benjamin. "The thing can be accomplished more easily than at first appears. I tell you what it is, Benjamin," addressing himself to the boy, "when you are qualified for the office, I will give you my large volume of short-hand sermons, and the reading of these will improve your manner of sermonizing."

This uncle had recently come over from England, and was boarding in the family. He was a very intelligent man, quite a literary character for the times, and had been accustomed to take down the sermons to which he listened, in short-hand, until he had preserved a large manuscript volume of them, which he valued highly. It was this volume which he promised to bequeath to his nephew when he should become qualified to enter the ministry.

This interview occurred almost one hundred and fifty years ago, between Benjamin Franklin, who paid too much for the whistle, and his father, whose Christian name was Josiah. The lad was eight years old at the time, a bright, active, intelligent boy, who was more fond of reading than any other child in the family. He was born in Boston, on Sunday, January 6 (Old Style, corresponding to January 17, New Style), 1706, and on the same day was carried into the Old South Church, and there baptized. Both his father and mother were members of that church.

If you ask how it is known that he was born and baptized on the same day, we answer, that on the "Old Boston Town Records of Births," under the heading, "Boston Births, entered 1708," is the following:—

> "Benjamin, son of Josiah Franklin, and Abiah, his wife, Born 6 Jan. 1706."

By some oversight or negligence the birth was not recorded until two years after Benjamin was born; yet it shows that he was born on Jan. 6, 1706.

Then we turn to the records of the Old South Church, and find among the baptism of infants the following:—

> "1706, Jan. 6, Benjamin, son of Josiah and Abiah Franklin."

Putting these two records together, they establish beyond doubt the fact that Benjamin Franklin was born and baptized on the same day. It has generally been said that we do not know by whom he was baptized, although the rite must have been performed either by Dr. Samuel Willard, or Rev. Ebenezer Pemberton, who were then pastors of the Old South Church. But the fact that the record is made in the handwriting of Dr. Willard would indicate that he baptized him. He was born in Milk Street, opposite the church, so that he had only to be carried across the street to receive the ordinance of baptism.

A picture of the old house in which he was born has been preserved, and it stood on the spot where now rises a lofty granite warehouse, bearing, in raised letters beneath the cornice, the inscription, "BIRTHPLACE OF FRANKLIN." The house measured twenty feet in width, and was about thirty feet long. It was three stories high in appearance, the third being the attic. On the lower floor of the main house there was only one room, which was about twenty feet square, and served the family for the triple purpose of parlour, sitting-room, and dining-hall. It contained an old-fashioned fireplace, so large that an ox might have been roasted before it. The second and third stories originally contained but one chamber each, of ample dimensions, and furnished in the plainest manner. The attic was an unplastered room, where probably some of the elder children lodged. This house stood about a hundred years after the Franklins left it, and was finally destroyed by fire, on Saturday, Dec. 29, 1810.

He was named after the aforesaid uncle, and this circumstance alone was well suited to beget a mutual interest and attachment between them. His love of books early attracted the attention of his parents and others, and they regarded him as a precocious child. On this account the remark was often volunteered, "that he ought to be sent to college."

We have said that Mr. Franklin was playing upon his violin on the evening of the aforesaid interview. He was very fond of music, was a good singer, and performed well upon the violin. He was wont to gather his family around him during the leisure hours of evening, and sing and play. Many cheerful and happy seasons were passed in this way at the fireside, the influence of which was excellent upon his children.

That it would be doubtful whether he could meet the expense of sending Benjamin to college, must appear to the reader, when he learns that he was a labouring man, and had a family of seventeen children, thirteen of whom sat around his table together at one time. Fourteen were older than Benjamin, and two were younger. To support so large a family must have taxed the energies of the father to the utmost, even though no one of them was destined for a learned profession.

It was arranged that Benjamin should immediately enter school, and enjoy the best literary advantages which the poverty of his father could provide. He acceded to the plan with hearty good-will, and commenced his studies with a zeal and enthusiasm such as few scholars exhibit.

The school was taught by Mr. Nathaniel Williams, successor of the famous Boston teacher, Mr. Ezekiel Cheever, who was instructor thirty-five years, and who discontinued teaching, as Cotton Mather said, "only when mortality took him off." The homely old wooden school-house, one story and a half high, stood near by the spot on which the bronze statue of Franklin is now seen, and there was the "school-house green," where "Ben" and his companions sported together. It was probably the only free grammar-school which Boston afforded at that time; for it was only a little village compared with its present size. It then contained only about ten thousand inhabitants, and now it has more than fifteen times that number. There were no stately public buildings at that time, like the State-house, Court-house, Custom-house, Athenæum, Public Library, etc. Such splendid granite blocks of stores as we now behold on almost every business street, were then unknown; and no shops could be found, as now, filled with the fabrics of every land. There were no costly houses of worship, the "Old South Meeting-house," then about half its present size, being the oldest one in existence at the time.

When Benjamin was born, the streets of Boston were not named. This was not done until the year after, when there were but one hundred and ten of them in number. Now there are a thousand streets, courts, and places. Thus it will be seen that the Boston of that day resembled the present Boston little more than Benjamin Franklin blowing his whistle resembled Benjamin Franklin the great statesman and philosopher.

"I have seen the teacher to-day," said Mr. Franklin to his wife, two or three months after his son entered school, "and he says that he is making rapid progress, and will soon stand first in his class, although others have enjoyed much better advantages."

"I am glad to hear it," answered Mrs. Franklin, with a satisfied air, such as mothers are likely to betray when they know that their children are doing well; "I think he will make a good scholar if he can have the opportunity, though I scarcely see how you will be able to educate him."

"I can hardly see how myself," said her husband; "yet I trust that God will provide a way. At any rate, I hope for the best."

"It will be more and more expensive every year to support him," added Mrs. Franklin, "since his clothes will cost more as he advances in years. The least expense in educating him we are having now."

"That is very true, and I have looked at the matter in this light, all the while not being able to see my way quite clear, yet trusting to Providence for a happy issue."

"It is well to trust in Providence if it is not done blindly, for Providence sometimes does wonders for those who trust. It is quite certain that He who parted the waters of the Red Sea for the children of Israel to pass, and fed them with manna from the skies, can provide a way for our Benjamin to be educated. But it looks to me as if some of his bread would have to drop down from heaven."

"Well, if it comes, that is enough," responded Mr. Franklin, rather drily. "If God does anything for him, he will do it in his own time and way. I shall be satisfied to see him qualified for usefulness in the service of the Church."

Within a few months after Benjamin entered school, he had advanced from the middle to the head of his class. He was so apt to learn, and gave so close attention to his lessons, that his teacher spoke of him as a boy of uncommon promise. He did not stand at the head of his class long, however, before he was transferred to a higher one. He so far outstripped his companions that the teacher was obliged to advance him thus, otherwise his mental progress would have been injuriously retarded. His parents were highly gratified with his diligent improvement of time and opportunities, and other relatives and friends began to prophesy his future eminence.

It is generally the case that such early attention to studies, in connection with the advancement that follows, awakens high hopes of the young in the hearts of all observers. Such things foreshadow the future character, so that people think they can tell what the man will be from what the boy is. So it was with young Benjamin Franklin. So it was with Daniel Webster,—his mother inferred from his close attention to reading, and his remarkable progress in learning, that he would become a distinguished man, and so expressed herself to others. She lived to see him rise in his profession, until he became a member of Congress, though she died before he reached the zenith of his renown. The same was true of David Rittenhouse, the famous mathematician. When he was but eight years old he constructed various articles, such as a miniature water-wheel, and at seventeen years of age he made a clock. His younger brother relates that he was accustomed to stop when he was ploughing in the field, and solve problems on the fence, and sometimes cover the plough-handles over with figures. The highest expectations of his friends were more than realized in his after life. The peculiar genius which he exhibited in his boyhood gave him fame at last. Again, George Stephenson, the great engineer, the son of a very poor man, who fired the engine at the Wylam Colliery, began his life labour when a mere boy. Besides watching the cows, and barring the gates at night after the coal waggons had passed, at twopence a day, he amused himself during his leisure moments in making clay engines, in imitation of that which his father tended. Although he lived in such humble circumstances that he was almost entirely unnoticed, yet it would have been apparent to any observer, that his intense interest in, and taste for, such mechanical work, evinced what the future man would be.

It was quite natural, then, for the parents and friends of Benjamin Franklin to be encouraged by his love of books, and diligent attention, especially when so much intellectual brightness was also manifest. The sequel will prove whether their hopes were wisely cherished.

CHAPTER III.

A CHANGE.

BENJAMIN had not been in school quite a year, when his father saw plainly that he would not be able to defray the expense of educating him.

"I might keep him along for the present," said he to his wife, "but I am satisfied that I cannot carry him through. My family expenses are now very great, and they will be still larger. It will make considerable difference in my expenses whether Benjamin is kept at school, or assists me by the labour of his hands."

"I am not surprised at all at your conclusion," replied Mrs. Franklin. "It is no more than I have expected, as I have before intimated. Parents must be better off than we are to be able to send a son to college."

"If they have as many children to support, you might add," said Mr. Franklin. "I could easily accomplish it with no larger family on my hands than some of my neighbours have."

"Do you intend to take Benjamin away from school at once?"

"Yes! I have very reluctantly come to the conclusion that I must. It is contrary to all my desires, but necessity compels me to do it."

"I am sorry for Benjamin," continued Mrs. Franklin, "for he has become much interested in his school, and it will be a great disappointment to him."

"I thought of that much before coming to my present decision; but there is no alternative. Providence seems to indicate, now, the course I should take, and I am the more willing to follow, because the times do not hold out so much encouragement to those who would enter the service of the Church. There are many trials and hardships to be met in the work, and at the present day, they seem to be peculiar."

"There are trials almost anywhere in these times," said Mrs. Franklin, "and I suppose we ought to bear them with fortitude. So far as that is concerned, I think Benjamin will not escape them, let him follow what business he may."

"True, very true, and I trust that I desire to place him where God would have me; but he has certainly hedged up his way to the ministry."

This subject was very thoroughly considered before it was opened to Benjamin. His father was too anxious to educate him to change his purpose without much patient thought and circumspection. Nothing but absolute necessity induced him to come to this decision. The hard hand of poverty was laid upon him, and he must have "bread before learning" for his children.

One evening, as the school term was drawing to a close, Mr. Franklin said to Benjamin—

"I think I shall be under the necessity of taking you away from school at the close of the term. The times are so hard, that I find, with my best exertions, I can do little more than supply you with food and clothes."

"And not go to school any more?" anxiously inquired Benjamin.

"Perhaps not. Such appears to be your prospect now, though I cannot say that God may not open a way hereafter; I hope he will. You are but nine years old, and there is time yet for a way to be provided."

"Why can I not attend school till I am old enough to help you?"

"You are old enough to help me now. I could find a plenty for you to do every day, so that you could make yourself very useful."

In those days boys were put to work much earlier than they are now. They had very small opportunities for acquiring knowledge, and the boys who did not go to school after they were ten years old were more in number than those who did. Besides, the schools were very poor in comparison with those of the present age. They offered very limited advantages to the young. It was not unusual, therefore, for lads as young as Benjamin to be made to work.

"But I do not intend to set you to work immediately," continued Mr. Franklin. "You ought to give some attention to penmanship and arithmetic, and I shall send you to Mr. Brownwell's writing-school for a season."

"I shall like that, for I want to know how to write well. Some of the boys no older than I am have been to his school some time."

"It is equally important that you learn to cipher, and Mr. Brownwell is an excellent teacher of arithmetic. It will not take you many months to become a good penman under his tuition, and to acquire considerable knowledge of numbers."

"I care more about writing than I do about arithmetic," said Benjamin. "I don't think I shall like arithmetic very well."

"Boys have to study some things they don't like," responded his father. "It is the only way they can qualify themselves for usefulness. You would not make much of an appearance in the world without some acquaintance with numbers."

"I know that," said Benjamin; "and I shall try to master it, even if I do not like it. I am willing to do what you think is best."

"I hope you will always be as willing to yield to my judgment. It is a good sign for a boy to accept cheerfully the plans of his father, who has had more experience."

Benjamin was generally very prompt to obey his parents, even when he did not exactly see the necessity of their commands. He understood full well that obedience was a law of the household, which could not be violated with impunity; therefore he wisely obeyed. His father was a religious man, puritanical and even severe in his views and habits; a walk was never allowed on Sunday, and "going to meeting" was one of the inexorable rules of the family.

Benjamin was reared under such family regulations. He was expected to regard them with becoming filial respect. Nor did he grow restless and impatient under them, nor cherish less affection for his father in consequence. We have no reason to believe that he sought to evade them; and there is no doubt that the influence of such discipline was good in forming his character. He certainly loved and respected his father as long as he lived. Many years thereafter, when his father was old and infirm, he was wont to perform frequent journeys from Philadelphia to Boston, to visit him. It was on one of these journeys that he rebuked the inquisitiveness of a landlord, by requesting him, as soon as he entered his tavern, to assemble all the members of his family together, as he had something important to communicate. The landlord proceeded to gratify him, and as soon as they were brought together in one room, he said, "My name is Benjamin Franklin; I am a printer by trade; I live, when at home, in Philadelphia; in Boston I have a father, a good old man, who taught me, when I was a boy, to read my book, and say my prayers; I have ever since thought it was my duty to visit and pay my respects to such a father, and I am on that errand to Boston now. This is all I can recollect at present of myself that I think worth telling you. But if you can think of anything else that you wish to know about me, I beg you to out with it at once, that I may answer, and so give you an opportunity to get me something to eat, for I long to be on my journey that I may return as soon as possible to my family and business, where I most of all delight to be." This was a keen rebuke to a landlord who was disposed to be inquisitive, and interrogate his guests in an ungentlemanly way. But we have cited the incident to show that the filial love and respect which Benjamin had for his parents continued as long as they lived. The last act of affection and reverence that he could possibly perform to them was cheerfully made. It was the erection of a marble stone over their remains in Boston, bearing the following inscription:—

> "JOSIAH FRANKLIN
> And
> ABIAH his wife
> Lie here interred.
> They lived lovingly together in wedlock
> Fifty-five years;
> And without an estate, or any gainful employment,
> By constant labour, and honest industry
> (With God's blessing)
> Maintained a large family comfortably;
> And brought up thirteen children and seven grandchildren
> Reputably.
> From this instance, reader,
> Be encouraged to diligence in thy calling,
> And distrust not Providence.
> He was a pious and prudent man,
> She a discreet and virtuous woman.
> Their youngest son,
> In filial regard to their memory,
> Places this stone.
> J. F. born 1645; died 1744. Æt. 89.
> A. F. born 1667; died 1752. Æt. 85."

This stone had become so dilapidated in 1827, that the citizens of Boston supplied its place with a granite obelisk, on which the foregoing inscription may still be read.

It is good for boys, who are very likely to want their own way, to be obliged to obey exact rules in the family. It is a restraint upon their evil tendencies that tells well upon their riper years. It was to such an influence that Sir Robert Peel felt much indebted for his success in life. As an illustration of the obedience he was obliged to practise, in common with his brothers, he relates, that, in his youth, a comrade called one day to solicit their company upon some excursion. He was a young man of handsome address, intelligent, smart, and promising, though quite accustomed to enjoy much pastime. He was a fashionable young man for the times, wearing "dark brown hair, tied behind with blue ribbon; clear, mirthful eyes; boots which reached above his knees; a broad-skirted, scarlet coat, with gold lace on the cuffs, the collar, and the skirts; and a long waistcoat of blue silk. His breeches were buckskin; his hat was three-cornered, set jauntily higher on the right than on the left side." His name was Harry Garland. To his request that William, Edmund, and Robert might go with him, their father replied, "No, they cannot go out." Although the boys earnestly desired to go, they dared say nothing against their father's emphatic "No." He had work for them to do, and he never allowed pleasure to usurp the time for labour. The result is recorded on the page of English history. The three brothers of the Peel family became renowned in their country's brilliant progress. Harry Garland, the idle, foppish youth, became a ruined spendthrift. In this way the language of inspiration is verified. "Honour thy father and mother (which is the first commandment with promise), that it may be well with thee." The providence of God appears to make it well with the children who obey the commandment. Not the least of their reward is the respect and confidence of mankind which their obedience secures. Men universally admire to witness deeds that are prompted by true filial love. Such an act as that of the great engineer, George Stephenson, who took the first thirty pounds he possessed, saved from a year's wages, and paid off his blind old father's debts, and then removed both father and mother to a comfortable tenement at Killingworth, where he supported them by the labour of his hands, awakens our admiration, and leads us to expect that the Divine blessing will rest upon the author.

When the statue of Franklin was inaugurated, in 1856, a barouche appeared in the procession that carried eight brothers, all of whom received Franklin medals at the Mayhew School in their boyhood, sons of the late Mr. John Hall. They were all known to fame for their worth of character and wide influence. As the barouche in which they rode came into State Street, from Merchants' Row, these brothers all rose up in the carriage, uncovered their heads, and thus remained while passing a window at which their excellent and revered mother sat,—an act of filial regard so impressive and beautiful as to fill the hearts of beholders with profound respect for the affectionate sons.

Benjamin was taken away from school, agreeably to his father's decision, and sent to Mr. Brownwell, to perfect himself in arithmetic and penmanship. Less than a year he had attended the grammar-school, with little or no prospect of returning to his studies. But the disappointment was somewhat alleviated by the advantages offered at Mr. Brownwell's writing class. Here he made rapid progress in penmanship, though he failed in mastering the science of number. He had more taste, and perhaps tact, for penmanship than he had for arithmetical rules and problems, and this may account for the difference of his improvement in the two branches.

We should have remarked that Benjamin endeared himself to his teacher while he was a member of the public school, and it was with regret that the latter parted with his studious pupil. His close attention to his duties, and his habitual good deportment, in connection with his progress, made him such a scholar as teachers love.

CHAPTER IV.

MAKING CANDLES.

WHEN Benjamin was ten years old he had acquired all the education his father thought he could afford to give him. He could write a very good hand, and read fluently, though his knowledge of arithmetic was very limited indeed.

"Are you about ready, Benjamin, to come into the shop and help me?" inquired his father, at the dinner table.

"Am I not going to Mr. Brownwell's school any longer?" he asked, instead of replying to his father's question,—a Yankee-like way of doing things, truly.

"I think the close of this term will complete the education I am able to give you," replied his father. "You will fare, then, better than your brothers, in respect to schooling."

"I had rather not go into the shop," said Benjamin. "I think I shall not like to make candles, and I really wish you would engage in some other business."

"And starve, too," said his father. "In such times as these we must be willing to do what will insure us a livelihood. I know of no other business that would give me a living at present, certainly none that I am qualified to pursue."

Mr. Franklin was a dyer by trade, in England, and designed to continue it when he removed to America, about the year 1685. But he found, on arriving at Boston, that it would be quite impossible for him to support his family at this trade. The country was new, and the habits of the people were different from those of the English, so that the dyeing business could receive but little patronage. The next pursuit that presented itself, with fair promises of success, was that of "tallow-chandler and soap-boiler;" not so cleanly and popular a business as some, but yet necessary to be done, and very useful in its place; and this was enough for such a man as Mr. Franklin to know. He cared very little whether the trade was popular, so long as it was indispensable and useful. To him no business was dishonourable, if the wants of society absolutely demanded it.

"Well, I should rather make soap and candles than starve," said Benjamin; "but nothing else could make me willing to follow the business."

"One other thing ought to make you willing to do such work," added his father. "You had better do this than do nothing, for idleness is the parent of vice. Boys like you should be industrious, even if they do not earn their bread. It is better for them to work for nothing than not to work at all."

"I think they may save their strength till they can earn something," said Benjamin. "People must like to work better than I do, to work for nothing."

"You do not understand me," continued Mr. Franklin. "I mean to say, it is so important for the young to form industrious habits, that they had better work for nothing than to be idle. If they are idle when they are young, they will be so when they become men, and idleness will finally be their ruin. 'The devil tempts all other men, but idle men tempt the devil,' is an old and truthful proverb, and I hope you will never consent to verify it."

Mr. Franklin had been a close observer all his life, and he had noticed that industry was characteristic of those who accomplished anything commendable. Consequently he insisted that his children should have employment. He allowed no drones in his family hive. All had something to do as soon as they were old enough to toil. Under such influences Benjamin was reared, and he grew up to be as much in love with industry as his father was. Some of his best counsels, and most interesting sayings, when he became a man, related to this subject. The following are among the maxims which he uttered in his riper years:—

> "Sloth, like rust, consumes faster than labour wears; while the used key is always bright."
>
> "But dost thou love life? Then do not squander time, for that is the stuff life is made of."
>
> "If time be of all things the most precious, wasting time must be the greatest prodigality."
>
> "Sloth makes all things difficult, but industry all easy; and he that ariseth late must trot all day, and shall scarce overtake his business at night; while laziness travels so slowly, that poverty soon overtakes him."
>
> "At the working man's house hunger looks in, but dares not enter."
>
> "Diligence is the mother of good luck, and God gives all things to industry."
>
> "One to-day is worth two to-morrows."
>
> "Drive thy business, let not thy business drive thee."

"God helps them that help themselves."

These are very beautiful and expressive sentences, and they show that Benjamin Franklin thought as much of industry in his manhood as his father did a quarter of a century before. Take the first, in which he compares slothfulness to rust, which will consume iron tools or machinery faster than their constant use will. As the use of a hoe or a spade keeps it polished, so the habitual exercise of the powers of human nature preserves them in a good condition. A key that is cast aside soon rusts, and is spoiled, but "the used key is always bright." It is more fit for use because it has been used.

How true it is that "hunger dare not enter the working-man's house!" By the sweat of his brow he earns his daily bread, and his children do not cry with hunger. It is the lazy man's table that has no bread. His children rise up hungry, and go to bed supperless. God himself hath said, "If any would not work, neither should he eat."

"Diligence is the mother of good luck." Another gem of wisdom that commands our acquiescence. How common for the indolent to complain of "bad luck!" Their families need the necessaries of life, as both a scanty table and rent apparel bear witness, and they cast the blame upon "ill luck," "misfortune," "unavoidable circumstances," or something of the kind. Many men whose faces are reddened and blotched by intemperance, begotten in the barroom where they have worse than idled away days and weeks of precious time, are often heard to lament over their "bad luck," as if their laziness and intemperance were not the direct cause of their misery. But it is not often that the diligent experience "bad luck." They receive a reward for their labours, and thrift and honour attend their steps, according as it is written in the Bible: "The soul of the sluggard desireth, and *hath* nothing; but the soul of the diligent shall be made fat. Seest thou a man diligent in his business? he shall stand before kings; he shall not stand before mean men."

But we need not enlarge upon these sayings of Franklin. They are all charged with wisdom, and might be expanded into volumes. The more we study them, the more beauty we perceive.

It was settled that Benjamin should assist his father in the manufacture of candles, notwithstanding his disinclination to engage in the business. His prospects of more schooling were thus cut off at ten years of age, and now he was obliged to turn his attention to hard work. It was rather an unpromising future to a little boy. No more schooling after ten years of age! What small opportunities in comparison with those enjoyed by nearly every boy at the present day! Now they are just beginning to learn at this early age. From ten they can look forward to six or eight years of golden opportunities in the school-room. Does the young reader appreciate the privileges which he enjoys?

"To-morrow for the work-shop, Benjamin!" exclaimed Mr. Franklin, with a tone of pleasantry, on the evening before he was initiated into the mysteries of making candles. "I am full of business, and need another hand very much at present."

"You can't expect much help from me," said Benjamin, "till I learn how to do the work. So I am thinking you will continue to be hurried for a while, unless you have another hand besides me."

"You can do what I shall set you about just as well as a boy, or even a man, who had worked at the business for a year."

"I wonder what that can be, that is so easy!" added Benjamin, with some surprise.

"You can cut the wicks, fill the moulds for cast-candles, keep the shop in order, run hither and thither upon errands, and do other things that will save my time, and thus assist me just as much as a man could in doing the same things."

"I am sure," said Mrs. Franklin, who had been listening to the conversation attentively, "that is inducement enough for any boy, but a lazy one, to work. You can make yourself about as useful to your father as a man whom he would have to pay high wages."

"You will aid me just as much in going errands," said his father, "as in doing anything else. I have a good deal of such running to do, and if you do it, I can be employed in the more important part of my business, which no one else can attend to. Besides, your nimble feet can get over the ground much quicker than my older and clumsier ones, so that you can really perform this part of the business better than I can myself."

Benjamin made no reply to these last remarks, although he was more favourably impressed, after hearing them, with the tallow-chandler's calling. On the following day he entered upon his new vocation, and, if "variety is the spice of life," then his first day in the shop had a plenty of spice. The shop was situated at the corner of Hanover and Union Streets, having the sign of a large blue ball, bearing the inscription:

1698 JOSIAS
    FRANKLIN 1698.

He cut wicks, filled moulds, performed errands, and played the part of general waiter, in which there was much variety. And this was his work for successive weeks, very little of his time running to waste. Do you ask how he likes it? The following conversation with his mother will answer.

"I don't like it at all, mother,—no better than I thought I should," he said. "I wish I could do something else."

"What else is there for you to do, Benjamin?" replied his mother. "What would you like to do?"

"I would like to go to sea."

"Go to see what?" she inquired, as if she did not understand him at first.

"Go on a voyage to Europe, or the East Indies."

"What!" exclaimed his mother, exhibiting surprise, for she had not dreamed that her son had any inclination to go to sea. "Want to be a sailor? What put that into your head?"

"I have always thought I should like to go to sea," he answered; "and I am so tired of making candles that I want to go now more than ever."

"I am astonished, Benjamin. You might know that I should never give my consent to that. I should almost as lief bury you. And how can you want to leave your good home, and all your friends, to live in a ship, exposed to storms and death all the time?"

"It is not because I do not love my home and friends, but I have a desire to sail on a voyage to some other country. I like the water, and nothing would suit me so well as to be a cabin-boy."

"There, Benjamin, you must never say another word about it," continued his mother; "and you must not think any more about going; for I shall never give my consent, and I know *your father never will*. It was almost too much for me when your brother broke away from us, and went to sea. I could not pass through another such trial. So you must not persist in your wish, if you would not send me down to the grave." And here his mother alluded to one of the most bitter experiences of her life, when a son older than Benjamin became restless at home, and would not be persuaded from his purpose of going to sea. It caused her many unhappy hours.

Benjamin had said nothing about this matter to his father, and this prompt veto of his mother put a damper on his hopes, so that he continued to work at the shop, with all his dislike for the business. His parents talked over the matter, and his father was led thereby to watch him more carefully, that he might nip the first buddings of desire for the sea. At length, however, Benjamin ventured to make known his wishes to his father.

"I have thought," said he, "that I should like to go to sea, if you are willing;" and there he stopped, evidently expecting to be refused.

"What has happened to lead you to desire this?" inquired his father.

"Not anything," he answered. "I always thought I should like it,—though I have had a stronger desire lately."

"I see how it is," continued his father. "You have been to the water with the boys frequently of late, and I have noticed that you loved to be in a boat better than to make candles. I am afraid that your sports on the water are making you dissatisfied with your home, and that here is the secret of your wanting to go to sea."

"No, father; I think as much of my home as I ever did, and I like a boat no better now than I did the first time I got into one."

"Perhaps it is so; but boys don't always know when they are losing their attachment to home. You need not say another syllable, however, about going to sea, for I shall never consent to it. You may as well relinquish at once all thought of going, since I strictly forbid your laying any such plans. If you do not wish to be a tallow-chandler, you may try some other business. I shall not insist upon your working with me, though I shall insist upon your following some calling."

"I shall not want to go to sea against your wishes," said Benjamin. "I only thought I would go if you and mother were perfectly willing. I can work at this dirty trade, too, if you think it is best, though I can never like it."

"I am glad to see that you have so much regard for your parents' wishes," said his father. "If your brother had been as considerate, he never would have become a sailor. Children should always remember that their parents know best, as they have had more experience and time to observe. I say again, if you will abandon all thoughts of a seafaring life, I will try to find you a situation to learn some trade you may choose for yourself."

Benjamin was not disposed to enter upon a sailor's life contrary to his parents' counsels, and he submitted to his father's decision with as much cheerfulness and good feeling as could be expected in the circumstances. He knew that it was little use to tease his father when he said "no" to a project. His emphatic "no" usually put an end to all controversy.

There is little doubt that Benjamin had been somewhat influenced by his frolics in and on the water. For some time, as opportunity offered, he had been down to the water both to bathe and take boat-rides. He had become an expert swimmer in a very short time, and not one of the boys so readily learned to manage a boat. He exhibited so much tact in these water feats, that he was usually regarded as a leader by the boys, and all matters of importance were referred to his judgment. It was not strange that he should be more in love with an ocean life after such pastimes with his comrades. Whether he admitted it or not, it is probable that his desire to go to sea was greatly increased by these pleasant times in and on the water.

It was certainly a poor prospect that was before the young tallow-chandler. It was not a trade to call into exercise the higher and nobler faculties of the mind and heart. On that account, no one could expect that Benjamin would rise to much distinction in the world; and this will serve to awaken the reader's surprise as he becomes acquainted with the sequel. A little fellow, ten or twelve years of age, cutting the wicks of candles, and filling the moulds, does not promise to become a great statesman and philosopher. Yet with no more promise than this some of the most distinguished men commenced their career. Behold Giotti, as he tends his father's flock, tracing the first sketches of the divine art in the sand with a clumsy stick,— a deed so unimportant that it foreshadowed to no one his future eminence. See Daniel Webster, the great expounder of the American Constitution, sitting, in his boyhood, upon a log in his father's mill, and studying portions of that Constitution which were printed upon a new pocket-handkerchief; a trivial incident at the time, but now bearing an important relation to that period of his life when his fame extended to every land. Recall the early life of Roger Sherman, bound as an apprentice to a shoemaker in consequence of his father's poverty, with little education and no ancestral fame to assist him,—how exceeding small the promise that his name would yet be prominent in his country's history! In like manner, the little candle-making lad of Boston, in 1717, scarcely appears to be related to the philosopher and statesman of the same name, in 1775. But the hand of God is in the lives of men as really as in the history of nations.

The reader should not make use of the fact that Franklin, and other eminent men, enjoyed small opportunities to acquire knowledge, as a plea that he himself need not be kept in school for a series of years. It is true that a little mental improvement may work wonders for a person in some circumstances, and it should lead us to inquire, if a little will accomplish so much, what will greater advantages do for him? A very little knowledge of electricity once saved the life of Benjamin Russell in his youth. He was an eminent citizen of Boston, born in the year 1761, and in his younger years he had learned from the writings of Franklin, who had become a philosopher, that it was dangerous to take shelter, during a thunder-shower, under a tree, or in a building not protected with lightning-rods. One day, in company with several associates, he was overtaken by a tempest, and some of the number proposed that they should take shelter under a large tree near by, while others advised to enter a neighbouring barn. But young Russell opposed both plans, and counselled going under a large projecting rock as the safest place. The result showed that a little knowledge of electricity was of great service to him; for both the barn and the tree were struck by lightning. But neither Benjamin Russell, nor any one else, from that day to this, would think of saying that there is no need of knowing much about electricity, since a little knowledge of it will do so much good. They might say it as reasonably, however, as a youth can say that there is no need of much schooling, since Benjamin Franklin, and others, became honoured and useful though they did not go to school after ten or twelve years of age. The deep regret of all this class of influential men ever has been, that their early advantages were so limited. George Stephenson, who did not learn to read until he was eighteen years old, felt so keenly on this point, that, when his own son became old enough to attend school, he sat up nights and mended the shoes and clocks of his neighbours, after having completed his day's labour, to obtain the means of educating him.

The Rogue's Wharf.—See page 44.

CHAPTER V.

THE ROGUE'S WHARF.

"ALL aboard!" exclaimed Benjamin, and so saying he bounded into the boat that lay at the water's edge. "Now for a ride: only hurry up, and make the oars fly;" and several boys leaped in after him from the shaking, trampled quagmire on which they stood.

"We shall be heels over head in mud yet," said one of the number, "unless we try to improve the marsh. There is certainly danger that we shall go through that shaky place, and I scarcely know when we shall stop, if we begin to go down."

"Let us build a wharf," said Benjamin, "and that will get rid of the quagmire. It won't be a long job, if all take hold."

"Where will you get your lumber?" inquired John.

"Nowhere. We don't want any lumber, for stones are better," answered Benjamin.

"It is worse yet to bring stones so far, and enough of them," added John. "You must like to lift better than I do, to strain yourself in tugging stones here."

"Look there," continued Benjamin, pointing to a heap of stones only a few rods distant. "There are stones enough for our purpose, and one or two hours is all the time we want to build a wharf with them."

"But those stones belong to the man who is preparing to build a house there," said Fred. "The workmen are busy there now."

"That may all be," said Benjamin, "but they can afford to lend them to us awhile. They will be just as good for their use after we have done with them."

"Then you expect they will lend them to you, I perceive; but you'll be mistaken," answered Fred.

"My mode of borrowing them is this,—we will go this evening, after the workmen have gone home, and tug them over here, and make the wharf long before bedtime;" and Benjamin looked queerly as he said it.

"And get ourselves into trouble thereby," replied another boy. "I will agree to do it if you will bear all the blame of stealing them."

"Stealing!" exclaimed Benjamin. "It is not stealing to take such worthless things as stones. A man couldn't sell an acre of them for a copper."

"Well, anyhow, the men who have had the labour of drawing them there won't thank you for taking them."

"I don't ask them to thank me. I don't think the act deserves any thanks," and a roguish twinkle of the eye showed that he knew he was doing wrong. And he added, "I reckon it will be a joke on the workmen to-morrow morning to find their pile of stones missing."

"Let us do it," said John, who was taken with the idea of playing off a joke. "I will do my part to carry the thing through."

"And I will do mine," said another; and by this time all were willing to follow the example of Benjamin, their leader. Perhaps all were afraid to say "No," according to the dictates of conscience, now that the enterprise was indorsed by one or two of their number. Boys are too often disposed to go "with the multitude to do evil." They are often too cowardly to do what they know is right.

The salt marsh, bounding a part of the millpond where their boat lay, was trampled into a complete quagmire. The boys were accustomed to fish there at high water, and so many feet, so often treading on the spot, reduced it to a very soft condition. It was over this miry marsh that they proposed to build a wharf.

The evening was soon there, and the boys came together on their rogue's errand. They surveyed the pile of stones, and found it ample for their purpose, though it looked like a formidable piece of work to move them.

"Some of them are bigger than two of us can lift," said Fred.

"Then three of us can hitch to and carry them," said Benjamin. "They must all be worked into a wharf this evening. Let us begin,—there is no time to lose."

"The largest must go first," said John. "They are capital ones for the foundation. Come, two or three must take hold of this," at the same time laying hold of one of the largest.

So they went to work with decided perseverance (the only commendable thing about the transaction), sometimes three or four of them working away at one stone, lifting and rolling it along. Benjamin was never half so zealous in cutting candle-wicks as he was in perpetrating this censurable act. He was second to no one of the number in cheerful active service on this occasion.

The evening was not spent when the last stone was carried away, and the wharf was finished,—a work of art that answered their purpose very well, though it was not quite so imposing as Commercial Wharf is now, and was not calculated to receive the cargo of a very large Liverpool packet.

"What a capital place it makes for fishing!" exclaimed Fred. "It is worth all it cost for that."

"Perhaps it will cost more than you think for before we get through with it," said John. "We can tell better about that when the workmen find their stones among the missing."

"I should like to hear what they will say," responded Benjamin, "when they discover what we have done, though I hardly think they will pay us much of a compliment. But I must hurry home, or I shall have trouble there. Come on, boys, let us go."

At this they hastened to their homes, not designing to make known the labours of the evening, if they could possibly avoid interrogation. They knew that their parents would disapprove of the deed, and that no excuse could shield them from merited censure. It was not strange, then, that they were both afraid and ashamed to tell of what they had done. But we will let twenty-four hours pass. On the following evening, when Mr. Franklin took his seat at his fireside, Benjamin had taken his book and was reading.

"Benjamin," said his father, "where was you last evening?"

Benjamin knew by his father's anxious look that there was trouble. He imagined that he had heard of their enterprise on the previous evening. After some hesitation, he answered, "I was down to the water."

"What was you doing there?"

"We were fixing up a place for the boat."

"See that you tell the truth, Benjamin, and withhold nothing. I wish to know what you did there."

"We built a wharf."

"What had you to build it with?"

"We built it of stones."

"And where did you get your stones?"

"There was a pile of them close by."

"Did they belong to you?"

"I suppose not."

"Did you not know that they belonged to the man who is building the house?"

"Yes, sir."

"Then you deliberately resolved to steal them, did you?"

"It isn't stealing to take stones."

"Why, then, did you take them in the evening, after the workmen had gone home? Why did you not go after them when the workmen were all there?"

Benjamin saw that he was fairly caught, and that, bright as he was, he could not get out of so bad a scrape unblamed. So he hung his head, and did not answer his father's last question.

"I see plainly how it is," continued his father; "it is the consequence of going out in the evening with the boys, which I must hereafter forbid. I have been willing that you should go out occasionally, because I have thought it might be better for you than so much reading. But you have now betrayed my confidence, and I am satisfied more than ever that boys should be at home in the evening, trying to improve their minds. You have been guilty of an act that is, quite flagrant, although it may have been done thoughtlessly. You should have known better, after having received so much good instruction as you have had at home."

"I did know better," frankly confessed Benjamin.

"And that makes your guilt so much the greater," added his father. "Do you think you will learn a lesson from this, and never do the like again?"

"I will promise that I never will."

Thus frankly did Benjamin confess his wrong, and ever after look upon that act with regret. In mature age he referred to it, and called it one of the first evil acts of his life. It was the second time he *paid too dear for his whistle*.

If seems that the workmen missed their stones, when they first reached the spot in the morning, and they soon discovered them nicely laid into a wharf. The proprietor was indignant, and exerted himself to learn who were the authors of the deed, and in the course of the day he gained the information, and went directly, and very properly, to their parents, to enter complaint. Thus all the boys were exposed, and received just rebuke for their misdemeanor. Benjamin was convinced, as he said of it many years afterwards, "that that which is not honest, could not be truly useful."

We have referred to Benjamin's habit of reading. It had been his custom to spend his evenings, and other leisure moments, in reading. He was much pleased with voyages, and such writings as John Bunyan's. The first books he possessed were the works of Bunyan, in separate little volumes. After becoming familiar with them, he sold them in order to obtain the means to buy "Burton's Historical Collections," which were small, cheap books, forty volumes in all. His father, also, possessed a good number of books for those times, when books were rare, and these he read through, although most of them were really beyond his years, being controversial writings upon theology. His love of reading was so great, that he even read works of this character with a degree of interest. In the library, however, were three or four books of somewhat different character. There was "Plutarch's Lives," in which he was deeply interested; also Defoe's "Essay on Projects." But to no one book was he more indebted than to Dr. Mather's "Essay to do Good." From this he derived hints and sentiments which had a beneficial influence upon his after life. He said, forty or fifty years afterwards, "It gave me a turn of thinking that had an influence on some of the principal future events of my life." And he wrote to a son of Cotton Mather, "I have always set a greater value on the character of a doer of good, than on any other kind of reputation; and if I have been, as you seem to think, a useful citizen, the public owes the advantage of it to that book." Some of the sentiments of the book which particularly impressed him were as follows: "It is possible that the wisdom of a poor man may start a proposal that may save a city, save a nation." "A mean (humble) mechanic,—who can tell what an engine of good he may be, if humbly and wisely applied unto it?" "The remembrance of having been the man that first moved a good law, were better than a statue erected for one's memory." These, and similar thoughts, stimulated his mind to action, and really caused him to attempt what otherwise would have been impossible.

If Benjamin had been engaged as usual, in reading, on that unfortunate evening, he would have escaped the guilt of an act that turned out to be a serious matter rather than a joke. The habit of spending leisure hours in poring over books, has saved many boys from vice and ruin. Many more might have been saved, if they had been so fond of books as to stay at home evenings to read. It is an excellent habit to form, and tends to preserve the character unsullied, while it stores the mind with useful knowledge.

We shall see, as we advance, that Benjamin became very systematic and economical in the use of his time, that he might command every moment possible to read. The benefit he derived from the exercise when he was young caused him to address the following letter, many years thereafter, to a bright, intelligent girl of his acquaintance. The letter, being devoted to "*Advice on Reading*," is a valuable one to young persons now.

> "I send my good girl the books I mentioned to her last night. I beg of her to accept of them as a small mark of my

esteem and friendship. They are written in the familiar, easy manner for which the French are so remarkable, and afford a good deal of philosophic and practical knowledge, unembarrassed with the dry mathematics used by more exact reasoners, but which is apt to discourage young beginners.

"I would advise you to read with a pen in your hand, and enter in a little book short hints of what you find that is curious, or that may be useful; for this will be the best method of imprinting such particulars on your memory, where they will be ready either for practice on some future occasion, if they are matters of utility, or, at least, to adorn and improve your conversation, if they are rather points of curiosity; and, as many of the terms of science are such as you cannot have met with in your common reading, and may therefore be unacquainted with, I think it would be well for you to have a good dictionary at hand, to consult immediately when you meet with a word you do not comprehend the precise meaning of.

"This may, at first, seem troublesome and interrupting; but it is a trouble that will daily diminish, as you will daily find less and less occasion for your dictionary, as you become more acquainted with the terms; and, in the meantime, you will read with more satisfaction, because with more understanding. When any point occurs in which you would be glad to have further information than your book affords you, I beg that you would not in the least apprehend that I should think it a trouble to receive and answer your questions. It will be a pleasure and no trouble. For though I may not be able, out of my own little stock of knowledge, to afford you what you require, I can easily direct you to the books where it may most readily be found. Adieu, and believe me ever, my dear friend,

"B. FRANKLIN."

CHAPTER VI.

TABLE TALK.

"YES," replied Mr. Franklin, to the inquiry of a friend who was dining with him; "my ancestors were inured to hardships, and I myself am not altogether a stranger to them. I had but little opportunity of going to school, and have always had to work hard for a livelihood."

"So much the better for you now," replied his friend; "for in this new country, and these hard times, you cannot find the support of a large family an easy matter."

"That is true; but I have never regretted coming to this country. The liberty of worshipping God according to the dictates of conscience, is one of the richest blessings, and more than compensates for the trial of leaving my native land."

"Then you experienced the rigours of intolerance there, in some measure, did you?"

"Oh yes; my forefathers adhered to the Protestant faith through the reign of Mary, and were often in great danger from the bitter hatred of the Papists. I sometimes wonder that they did not forfeit their lives in those days of persecution."

"I can relate to you one interesting fact," interrupted Uncle Benjamin, addressing himself to the guest. "Our ancestors possessed an English Bible, which they valued highly, of course; but there was danger of losing it, through the craftiness and hostility of the Papal powers. They held the Protestant Bible in absolute contempt. So, to conceal their Bible, at the same time they could enjoy the reading of it, they 'fastened it open with tapes under and within the cover of a joint-stool.' When our great-grandfather desired to read it to his family, according to his daily custom, 'he placed the joint-stool on his knees, and then turned over the leaves under the tapes.' While he was reading, one of the children was stationed at the door to give the alarm if he should see 'the apparitor coming, who was an officer of the spiritual court.' If the officer was seen approaching, the stool was immediately set down upon its feet, and the Bible in this way was concealed from view. For a considerable time they were obliged to read the Scriptures in this secret manner."

"But your father was not thus persecuted, was he?" inquired the friend.

"He was not persecuted to such a degree," answered Uncle Benjamin, "though he had some experience of this kind; and even brother Josias and myself did not escape. Our father's family continued in the Church of England till about the end of Charles the Second's reign, when Josias and I joined the Nonconformists, and subjected ourselves to much contempt."

"And that is the reason I am in this country now," said Mr. Franklin. "We enjoyed few privileges, and frequently our religious meetings were disturbed, as they were forbidden by law. On this account some of my acquaintances resolved to remove to this country, and I decided to join them."

"How long ago was that?"

"It was about 1685, so that you will perceive I am one of the old settlers of America. I have been here long enough to witness many changes, and have no desire to return to my native country. My children can scarcely appreciate how much they enjoy, in comparison with the experience of their ancestors."

Benjamin had often heard the last remark, as a reminder of his obligations to be good and useful. Indeed, this whole tale of persecution he had listened to over and over, and had heard his Uncle Benjamin tell the story of the Bible and stool a number of times. He had come to the conclusion that he was faring better than his father did, although he did not think his own lot remarkably flattering.

This conversation at the dinner-table was a specimen of what frequently occurred there in the way of remark. Mr. Franklin was gratified to have some intelligent friend at his table with him, that they might converse upon some useful topics, for the benefit of his children. When he had no guest at his table, he would call the attention of his children to some subject calculated to improve their minds, thinking, at the same time, that it would serve to draw off their attention from their humble fare. Children are apt to find fault with the food set before them, and perhaps the reader himself has more than once fretted over an unpalatable dish, and murmured for something else. Sometimes they beg for an article of food that is not on the table, declining to eat what is furnished for the family. It was not so at Mr. Franklin's table. He did not allow one of his children to complain of the food, however simple it might be; and his principal method of calling off their attention from the quality of their victuals was, as we have said, to converse upon some sensible theme. Their attention being directed to other things, they were seldom troubled about their food, and became almost indifferent to what was placed on the table. Benjamin said, in his manhood, on referring to this subject: "I am so unobservant of it, that to this day I can scarcely tell, a few hours after dinner, of what dishes it consisted. This has been a great convenience to me in travelling, where my companions have been sometimes very unhappy for the want of a suitable gratification of their more delicate, because better instructed tastes and appetites."

The guests of Mr. Franklin being usually intelligent, their conversation was instructive to the children, who acquired thereby many valuable items of information. The condition and prospects of the country, the oppressive measures of the English government, and the means of future prosperity, were among the topics which they heard discussed. Although it seems like a small, unimportant influence to bring to bear upon tender childhood, yet it left its mark upon their characters. They had more interest in the public questions of the day, and more general intelligence in consequence.

It is related of the Washburne family, of which four or five brothers occupy posts of political distinction in the United States, that in their early life their father's house was open to ministers, and was sometimes called "the minister's hotel." Mr. Washburne was a great friend of this class, and enjoyed their society much. At all times nearly, some one of the ministerial fraternity would be stopping there. His sons were thus brought into their society, and they listened to long discussions upon subjects of a scientific, political, and religious character, though public measures received a large share of attention. The boys acquired some valuable information by listening to their remarks, and this created a desire to read and learn more; and so they were started off in a career that bids fair to reflect honour both upon themselves and their country. Their early advantages were few, but the conversation of educated men, upon important subjects, laid the foundation of their eminence in public life.

"You must give heed to little things," Mr. Franklin would frequently say to his sons, when they appeared to think that he was too particular about some things, such as behaviour at the table, "although nothing can really be considered small that is important. It is of far more consequence how you behave, than what you wear."

Sometimes, if the meal was unusually plain (and it was never extravagant), he would say, "Many people are too particular about their victuals. They destroy their health by eating too much and too rich food. Plain, simple, wholesome fare is all that nature requires, and young persons who are brought up in this way will be best off in the end."

Such kind of remarks frequently greeted the ears of young Benjamin; so that, as we have already seen, he grew up without caring much about the kind of food which he ate. Perhaps here is to be found the origin of those rigidly temperate principles in both eating and drinking, for which he was distinguished all through his life. In his manhood, he wrote and talked upon the subject, and reduced his principles to practice. When he worked as a printer in England, his fellow-labourers were hard drinkers of strong beer, really believing that it was necessary to make them competent to endure fatigue. They were astonished to see a youth like Benjamin able to excel the smartest of them in the printing-office, while he drank only cold water, and they sneeringly called him "the Water-American."

The temperate habits which Benjamin formed in his youth were the more remarkable, because there were no temperance societies at that time, and it was generally supposed to be necessary to use intoxicating drinks. The evils of intemperance were not viewed with so much abhorrence as they are now, and the project of removing them from society was not entertained for a moment. Reformatory movements, in this respect, did not commence until nearly one hundred years after the time referred to. Yet Benjamin was fully persuaded in his youth that he ought to be temperate in all things. Probably there was not one of his associates who believed as he did on the subject. But he began early to think for himself, and this, with the excellent discipline of his wise and sagacious father, caused him to live in advance of those around him. It is not probable that he adopted the principle of total abstinence, and abstained entirely from the use of intoxicating drinks; but he was not in the habit of using it as a daily, indispensable beverage.

That the practice of Benjamin's father, to allow no finding fault with the food at the table, and to lead the way in profitable conversation, was a good one, we think no one can deny. It was very different, however, from much of the table-talk that is heard in families. Conversation is frequently brisk and lively, but it often runs in this way:—

"I don't want any of that, I don't like it," exclaimed Henry. "I should think you might have a better dinner than this."

"What would you have if you could get it,—roast chicken and plum pudding?" inquires his mother, laughing, instead of reproving him for his error.

"I would have something I can eat. You know I don't like that, and never did."

"Well, it does boys good, sometimes, to eat what they don't like, especially such particular ones as you are," says his father.

"I shan't eat what I don't like, at any rate," continues Henry, "I shall go hungry first."

"There, now," added his father, "let me hear no more complaint about your food. You are scarcely ever suited with your victuals."

"May I have some ——?" calling for some article not on the table.

"If you will hold your tongue, and get it yourself, you can have it."

"And let me have some, too!" shouts James, a younger brother; "I don't like this, neither. May I have some, father?"

"And I too," said Jane, setting up her plea. "I must have some if they do."

In this way the table-talk proceeds, until fretting, scolding, crying, make up the sum total of the conversation, and family joys are embittered for the remainder of the day. Finding fault with food is the occasion of all the unhappiness.

Let the reader ask himself how much he has contributed to make conversation at the table proper and instructive. Has he thought more of the quality of his food than of anything else at the family board? If the review of the past reveals an error in this respect, let him learn a valuable lesson from this part of Benjamin Franklin's life. Though it may seem to be an unimportant matter, accept the testimony of Benjamin himself, and believe that it leaves its impress upon the future character.

CHAPTER VII.

CHOOSING A TRADE.

"YOU will have to be a tallow-chandler, after all, when your brother gets married and goes away," said one of Benjamin's associates to him. He had heard that an older son of Mr. Franklin, who worked at the business with his father, was about to be married, and would remove to Rhode Island, and set up business for himself.

"Not I," replied Benjamin. "I shall work at it no longer than I am obliged to do."

"That may be, and you be obliged to work at it all your life. It will be, as your father says, till you are twenty-one years old."

"I know that; but my father does not desire to have me work in his shop against my wishes—only till I can find some other suitable employment. I would rather go to sea than anything."

"Are your parents not willing that you should go to sea?"

"No; they won't hear a word about it. I have talked with them till it is of no use. They seem to think that I should be shipwrecked, or that something else would happen, to prevent my return."

"Then, if you can't go to sea, and you won't be a tallow-chandler, what can you do?"

"I hardly know myself; but almost anything is preferable to this greasy business. If people had no more light than the candles I should make, unless I was obliged, they would have a pretty dark time of it."

"I don't think it is a very disagreeable business," continued his companion. "It is quite easy work, certainly,—much more to my liking than sawing wood, and some other things I could name."

"It may be easy," replied Benjamin; "but it is dirty and simple. It requires no ingenuity to do all that I do. Almost any simpleton could cut wicks and fill candle-moulds. A fellow who can't do it couldn't tell which side his bread is buttered. *I* prefer to do something that requires thought and ingenuity."

"There is something in that; but I guess it will take all your ingenuity to work yourself out of the tallow-chandler's business," responded his friend, rather dryly.

This conversation occurred one day in the shop, when Mr. Franklin was out. But just at this point he returned, and soon after the young visitor left. Benjamin was not acquainted with all his father's plans, and he had actually proceeded further than he was aware of towards introducing him into another calling, as the following conversation with Mrs. F., on the previous evening, will show—

"I have resolved to find some other employment for Benjamin at once," said he; "as John is to be married so soon, he will be able to render me but little more assistance, and I must have some one to take his place."

"Are you satisfied," inquired Mrs. Franklin, "that Benjamin cannot be prevailed upon to take the place of John in your shop?"

"Oh, yes! he is so dissatisfied with the business, that I fear he will yet go to sea, unless his attention is soon turned to some other pursuit. Then, if he has a taste for any other honourable pursuit, I am willing that he should follow it. He would not accomplish much at candle-making with his present feelings."

"Have you anything in view for him to do?" asked Mrs. F.

"Not positively. I want to learn, if I can, whether he has taste and tact for any particular business. If he has, he will accomplish more in that. I don't believe in compelling a boy to follow a pursuit for which he has no relish, unless it is where nothing else offers."

"I think it is very necessary for boys to have a definite trade," said Mrs. F.; "they are more likely to succeed than those who are changing often from one thing to another. 'A rolling stone gathers no moss,' is an old saying."

"That is the principal reason for my plan to introduce him into some other business soon. No one feels the importance of this more than I do, and I have pretty thoroughly imbued the mind of Benjamin with the same views. I think he has a desire to follow a definite calling, though now his taste seems to draw him towards a seafaring life."

Benjamin could have appreciated this last remark, if it had been uttered in his hearing. For he had listened to so much counsel upon this point, that he had no desire to run from one thing to another. And he continued to cherish this feeling. When he became a man, he wrote the following maxims, among the many of which he was the author:—

> "He that hath a trade hath an estate."

> "He that hath a calling hath an office of honour."

Here he taught the same lesson that he received from the lips of his father and mother when he was young. A trade is the assurance of a livelihood, however hard the times may be. As a general rule, they who follow trades secure a living, when they who have none come to want and suffer.

But to return. Mr. Franklin rather surprised Benjamin by saying, after his associate left the shop, "I have decided on finding some other business for you immediately, if possible. I hope to find some opening for your learning an agreeable trade."

"Where shall you go to find one?" inquired Benjamin, scarcely expecting to have his wishes gratified so early. "Have you any particular trade in view?"

"No; I want to consult your tastes about the matter first; and I propose to go to-morrow with you, to see what we can find."

"And I go with you, did you say?"

"Yes; I wish to have you witness some things to which I shall call your attention, and decide for yourself what calling to follow."

"Where will you go?" inquired Benjamin, deeply interested in the plan, as well he might be.

"I shall not go out of town. Boston furnishes good examples of the different trades, and we shall not be under the necessity of extending our researches beyond its limits. So to-morrow I think we will start."

Benjamin was delighted with the prospect of being delivered soon from the tallow-chandler's shop, and he anticipated the morrow with considerable impatience. He rejoiced when the light of the next morning came in at his chamber window, and brighter and earlier he was up to await his father's bidding. Suitable preparations were made, and directly after breakfast they set forth upon their important errand. The first shop they visited was that of a joiner, where he saw the plane and hammer used to advantage. He had witnessed such labour before, and also seen other employments to which his father called his attention on that day; but he never observed these different trades with the object which now brought him to the shops. Having spent some time at the joiner's bench, he next went to a turner's place of business, where he saw different articles turned to order, in so rapid a manner as to surprise him. He was more interested in the turning-lathe, and its rapid movement, than he was in the use of joiner's tools. Passing through a prominent street, after leaving the turner's, they came to an unfinished structure, on which bricklayers were employed. Here another trade was on exhibition, and Benjamin's attention was called to it, and the various kind of labour which this class of toilers were obliged to perform were explained to him. In this way they visited other work-shops, until they had seen the practical operations of the different trades, and Benjamin understood what kind of toil each required. One of the last shops they visited was that of Samuel Franklin, a son of Uncle Benjamin, and, of course, a cousin of Benjamin. He learned the trade of cutler in London, and had just come over and established himself in Boston. The business of a cutler is to make knives and other cutting instruments, in some respects a very interesting and attractive trade. Benjamin was evidently more pleased with this kind of business than any he had seen on that day. Whether it grew out of boyish love for jack-knives, or was the consequence of closely observing the ingenious modes of manufacturing cutlery, we need not say. It is enough to know that he was partially captivated by the trade, and before they reached home his father was well satisfied which trade he would select, though he had not questioned him at all on this point.

"What trade have you decided to follow, Benjamin?" inquired his mother, as they sat at the tea-table; and she let fall a most loving smile upon her boy.

"I think any of them are better than making candles," he replied, "although I like Samuel's trade the best of all."

"That is just what I expected," said his father, laughingly. "I saw that you fell in love with his work, and I think myself that it is a very pleasant and promising business."

"So you will decide to take that trade, will you?" said his mother.

"In preference to all the trades I have seen yet," said Benjamin.

"He is after a pocket knife," interrupted John, who sat at the table, speaking in a vein of pleasantry. "I see clearly what has taken *his* eye."

"I suppose John will never care more about a knife, now he is going to have a wife," added Mr. Franklin, addressing his remark to Benjamin, in order to help him out of the predicament into which John's remark had placed him. "But did you not like the brazier's business?"

"Yes, sir; I liked it very well, but not so well as I do the cutler's trade. If I can have my choice I shall choose that, and will begin to-morrow, if you are willing."

"I shall make no objection, if that is your decision," replied his father. "I want you should weigh the matter carefully, however, and not be hasty in choosing."

"It remains to be seen whether Samuel will take him as an apprentice," said Mrs. Franklin. "Perhaps he may not want one. He has just commenced, and cannot be doing much business yet."

"Father can easily learn that," said Benjamin. "He can see cousin Samuel to-morrow, and decide the matter at once."

"I will see him to-morrow," said his father, "and arrange for you to go into his shop if possible."

On the following day, Mr. Franklin called upon Samuel, his nephew, and made known the wishes of Benjamin. Although it was a new and unexpected subject, yet he received it favourably, and finally decided that Benjamin might come immediately, and try his hand at this new business. He thought it was best for both parties that no definite agreement or bargain should be made until Benjamin had tried the work, to which his father assented.

Accordingly, Benjamin entered upon his new trade immediately, and was much pleased with it. It was so different from the work of candle-making, and required so much more thought and ingenuity, that he was prepared to pronounce it "first rate." It was with a light and cheerful heart that he went to each day's task.

Mr. Franklin acted wisely in consulting the inclination of his son about a trade. A boy may have more qualifications for one pursuit than another; and this will generally be made manifest in the bent of his mind. He will exhibit a degree of tact for one calling, while he may be a blunderer at almost anything else. This characteristic is more remarkable with some boys than with others, and a disregard of it often entails unhappiness upon a whole family. When Handel, the distinguished musician, was a child, his father strictly forbade his listening to a note of music, or indulging his talent for the art. Although he exhibited remarkable musical abilities, his father paid no regard to the fact, but was determined to rear him to the profession of law. He ordered all musical instruments to be carried out of the house, and made it as difficult as possible for his son to gratify his taste for sweet sounds. But through the assistance of a servant, the boy obtained an instrument, which he kept in the garret; and there, when opportunity offered, with the strings of his "clavichord" so covered with pieces of cloth as to deaden the sound, he practised music until he became a proficient in harmony. It was not, however, until his father took him on a visit to see an elder brother, who was in the family of the Prince of Saxe-Weisenfels, that he became acquainted with the progress he had made in his loved art. While there he happened to go into the royal chapel just as the service was closing, when he glided up to the organ, unperceived, and commenced playing. The Prince was on the point of retiring; but he stopped, and inquired who was playing. He was told that it was young Handel, only seven years old; whereupon the Prince ordered the boy and his father to be summoned into his presence. The result of the interview was, that the Prince arranged for Handel to be placed for tuition under the organist of Halle Cathedral, where he soon became renowned. Posterity has not failed to condemn the unwise discipline of his father, in disregarding his inclination for a given pursuit.

When Sir Joshua Reynolds was a boy, he was inclined to embrace every opportunity to gratify his taste for drawing. His father had no sympathy with him in thus spending his time, and he sought to repress his aspirations of this kind. One day he discovered that Joshua had disfigured his exercise-book with a number of well-executed drawings; but, instead of encouraging his talents in this line, he sharply rebuked him, and wrote underneath the sketches, "*Done by Joshua out of pure idleness.*" His father was anxious that he should become a physician, and therefore he looked with no favour upon his propensity for drawing. But for the irrepressible power of genius, his unwise father would have deprived the world of one of its most gifted painters.

The father of John Smeaton pursued a like censurable course in the discipline of his son. He frowned upon those early developments of genius that foreshadowed the renowned engineer that he became. When only four or five years of age, he was often seen dividing circles and squares. He rejected the toys that other children used, preferring tools with which he could construct machines. When only six or seven years of age, he was discovered on the roof of the barn, much to the consternation of his father and mother, fixing up a windmill of his own construction. Soon afterwards having seen some men repairing a pump, he procured from them a piece of bored pipe, he made one of his own, with which he could raise water. At fourteen years of age he made an engine to turn rose-work, and many were his presents of boxes of wood and ivory turned by himself. He made all his tools for working wood, ivory, and metals. He also invented a lathe for cutting a perpetual screw in brass. And yet his father was determined to make a lawyer of him, and thus spoil the mechanic. He actually disregarded all these proofs of mechanical genius, and sent him to London to be educated for the bar; and it was not until his father began to see the impossibility of making a good attorney of him, that he consented to let him follow the profession which the bent of his genius plainly marked out.

The father of Benjamin Franklin acted more wisely in the first place, and resolved to educate him in that pursuit for which nature had best qualified him.

CHAPTER VIII.

THE PRINTER-BOY.

AFTER Benjamin had worked at cutlery a suitable time, his father went to close the bargain, and make out the papers for his apprenticeship. But, to his surprise, his nephew demanded such conditions that Mr. Franklin could not think of accepting his proposition; and the result was, that he took Benjamin away, much to his disappointment. The boy submitted to his father's decision, however, with true filial obedience, evidently believing that he had good reasons for taking such a stand. Now he was neither a tallow-chandler nor a cutler, though not destined to be long without employment.

Just before this juncture, as if Providence ordered events on Benjamin's account, his brother James returned from England, where he learned the printer's trade. He brought with him a good press, and type, in order to establish himself in Boston.

"How would you like to learn the printer's trade with your brother James?" inquired Mr. Franklin of Benjamin. "I have been thinking that it was a good thing you did not continue the cutlery business, because you have superior qualifications for this."

"What qualifications have I for this that I have not for the cutler's trade?" asked Benjamin.

"You are a good reader, and have an intellectual turn, being fond of books, and such things belonging to mental improvement as the trade of printer offers."

"I think I should like the business very well," added Benjamin. "Perhaps I should have a better opportunity to read than I should with cousin Samuel."

"Of course you would. For the very matter you may be required to put into type may be as interesting and profitable as anything you could find in a book. All that you read in books went through the printer's hand first."

"I had not thought of that before. I think I should like the business better than almost anything I know of. How long will it take to learn the trade?"

"It will take some time," answered Mr. Franklin. "You are now twelve years of age, and you can certainly acquire the best knowledge of the business by the time you are twenty-one years old."

"That is a long time," said Benjamin; "but I shall do what you think best."

"I want *you* should think it is best, too," said his father. "If you have no inclination to be a printer, I do not wish to have you undertake it. I have no confidence that you will succeed in any business for which you have no taste."

"Well, I think better of this business now than I do of any other," replied Benjamin, "and I should like to try it."

"I will speak with James about it," said his father, "and see what arrangements can be made. The prospects of the business are not very flattering at present, but I think the day is coming when it will thrive."

Mr. Franklin lost no time in consulting James, who favoured the plan without any reserve. He proposed to take Benjamin as an apprentice, to serve until he was twenty-one years of age, having only his board and clothes until the last year, when he would receive journeyman's wages. This was a good opportunity on the whole, for printing was in its infancy in America at that time. It is probable that not more than six or eight persons had been in the business in Boston before James Franklin commenced, in the year 1717. The demand for printing must have been very small indeed.

When Mr. Franklin first made known to Benjamin the conditions on which James would receive him into the printing-office, and that he would be expected to sign the indenture, and leave his father's roof for such a boarding-place as his brother might provide, he hesitated about taking the step. He stated his objections frankly and fully to his father, who removed them without much difficulty, so that the writings were drawn up, and Benjamin placed his signature to them and was henceforth a "Boston printer's boy."

He had not laboured long at the business before he was quite fascinated with it. He liked it better even than he expected. He exhibited, too, a good degree of tact for it, and his progress in learning the art was rapid. His brother was highly gratified with his close attention to his business, and commended him for the use he made of his leisure moments in reading. He was introduced now to another class of acquaintances, so that his opportunities for getting books to read were more favourable. The printing-office was frequented by booksellers' apprentices, whose employers necessarily wanted jobs of printing done. Through them Benjamin was made acquainted with the limited stock of books the market afforded.

"I will lend you that book to-night," said one of these apprentices to him, "if you will return it clean in the morning," alluding to a certain volume which Benjamin was looking over in the book-store.

"I should be glad to read it," answered Benjamin; "I think I can read it through before I go to bed, and so return it in the morning when I go to the office."

"You won't have much time left for sleep, if you read that book through before you go to bed," said the apprentice.

"Perhaps not; but I can afford to make a short night's rest of it, if I can have the reading of this book. I shall not mind that, and I can return it without a blemish."

"The book is for sale," continued the apprentice, "and we might have a call for it to-morrow, or I would let you keep it longer. If you do not read it all to-night, and we do not sell it to-morrow, you can take it home with you again to-morrow night. I frequently read a volume through, a little at a time, before we have a chance to sell it."

"You may be sure of having this in the morning, safe and sound," said Benjamin, as he left the store, thanking his friend for the kind favour.

He went home, and sat up most of the night to read the book, being more deeply interested in its contents than he was in pleasant dreams. A short nap, after the volume was finished, was all that time could afford him; and the bookseller got his book, and the printing-office its apprentice, in good season.

This was but a single instance of the favours he received in this way from his new acquaintances in the book business. Many nights he stole from sleep, that he might read volumes which he must return in the morning. In this way his mind was much improved, so that he began to be noticed in the office as a boy of great promise. One day Mr. Matthew Adams, a merchant of rank and influence, who had been attracted by Benjamin's appearance, said to him: "Do you find time to read any, with all the work you have to perform?"

"Yes, sir," replied Benjamin; "I read in the evenings, and occasionally find a little time during the day."

"It is an excellent plan for boys to improve their minds," said Mr. Adams; "you will never regret spending your time in this way. I should be glad to show you my library, and to lend you any books you may be interested to read."

"That is what I should like," said Benjamin, evidently delighted with this unexpected offer; "I find it difficult to get all the books I want."

"It would afford me great pleasure to assist you what little I can in this respect," repeated Mr. Adams. "Boys who are not privileged to go to school need such help, and I am glad to see that you are disposed to accept of it."

Benjamin thanked him for his kindness, and assured him that he should embrace the first opportunity to call at his house. He redeemed his promise at his earliest convenience, and Mr. Adams received him with genuine cordiality. He showed him his library, and allowed him to select any book he preferred to carry home, and invited him to come as often as he pleased for others. This was a brimful cup of kindness to Benjamin, and the reader may be sure that he thought highly of Mr. Adams. Nor was he backward in availing himself of the privilege offered, but went often to gratify his thirst for knowledge.

The reader can scarcely appreciate the value of this privilege to Benjamin, unless he understands that books were far from being abundant then. The bookstores, instead of being furnished with thousands of volumes to suit every taste in the reading world, offered only a meagre collection of volumes, such as would hardly be noticed at the present time. There were no large publishing houses, manufacturing many books in a year, and scattering them over the land, as is the case to-day. Neither were there any libraries at that time. The idea of a collection of books to lend for the public good had not entered the minds of men,—a striking contrast with this feature of society now, when a city like Boston opens its splendid Public Library of seventy-five thousand volumes, free to all her citizens, and smaller towns and villages throughout the land furnish reading matter for old and young in similar proportion; whilst private libraries of five, ten, twenty, and thirty thousand volumes are not unusual. Now, the trouble with boys is not how they can possibly get books to read, but what they shall select from the vast number that load the shelves of libraries and bookstores.

The habit of reading which Benjamin had thus early formed served to make him punctual. In order to command the more time, he was promptly at his work, and efficiently discharged every duty. He was seldom, if ever, caught in tardiness. It was this well-formed habit of punctuality that made him so reliable in the printing-office. His brother knew that he would be there at such a time, and that he would remain just so many hours. This fact won his confidence, as it does the confidence of every one. There is no quality that does more to gain a good name for an individual, and inspire the confidence of his fellow-men, than this one of punctuality. It is so generally found in company with other excellent traits of character, that it seems to be taken for granted, usually, that the punctual person is worthy in other respects. This quality contributed to the renown and influence of Lord Brougham, of whom it is said, that, when he was in the zenith of his glory, presiding in the House of Lords and the Court of Chancery, he found time to manage eight or ten public associations,—one of which was the Society for the Diffusion of Useful Knowledge,—and he was a pattern of punctuality in every place, being always in the chair when the hour for meeting arrived.

CHAPTER IX.

FIRST LITERARY ENTERPRISE.

"WHAT have you there?" inquired James, one day, looking over Benjamin's shoulder at some composition which he held in his hand. "Ay! poetry, is it? Then you are a poet, are you? Let me read it."

Benjamin rather hesitated to exhibit the first attempts of his muse to fly, but James was determined to read it, and so he gave it up to him, saying, "I was only seeing what I could do."

The fact was, Benjamin had been reading poetry, and, having a little of its spirit in his own nature, he was tempted to try his ability at writing some.

"That is really good," said James, after he had read it; "not quite equal to Virgil or Homer, but very good for a printer-boy to write. Have you any other pieces?"

"Two or three more," answered Benjamin, somewhat encouraged by his brother's commendation; "but they are not worth reading."

"Produce them," said James, "and I will tell you what they are worth." Whereupon Benjamin took two or three more from his pockets, which James read with evident satisfaction.

"I tell you what it is, Benjamin," said James after having read them all, "you can write something worth printing if you try; and if you will undertake it, you may print and sell a sheet in the streets. I have no doubt that it would sell well."

"I will see what I can do," replied Benjamin, "though I suspect my poetry won't read very well in print."

Benjamin was not long in producing two street ballads, better, perhaps, than anything he had written before, but still susceptible of very great improvement. One was entitled "The Lighthouse Tragedy," and was founded on the shipwreck of Captain Worthilake and his two daughters. The other was a sailor's song, on the capture of the famous "Teach," or "Bluebeard," the pirate. James read them with approbation.

"Now," said he, "you shall put them into type, and sell them about the town, if you are willing. I have no doubt that a good number of them may be disposed of."

"How many copies of them would you print?" inquired Benjamin.

"We can print a few to begin with, and let the type remain standing until we see how they go. Then we shall run no risk."

"Shall I do it immediately?"

"As soon as you can," answered James. "The quicker the better."

Benjamin was not long in printing the two ballads, and having them ready for sale. Under the direction of his brother, he went forth, in due time, to offer them about the town. Whether he cried them about the streets, as the newsboys do the daily papers now, we have no means of knowing. But he met with very good success, particularly in the sale of the first, "The Lighthouse Tragedy." That commemorated an event of recent occurrence, and which excited much public feeling and sympathy at the time, so that people were quite prepared to purchase. It sold even beyond his expectations, and his success inflated his vanity somewhat. It caused him to believe, almost, that he was a genuine poet, and that distinction and a fortune were before him. If he had not been confronted by his father on the subject, it is possible that the speculation might have proved a serious injury to him. But his father learned of his enterprise, and called him to an account. Perhaps he stepped into his shop, as he was selling them about town, and gave him a copy. At any rate, his father learned the fact, and the following interview will show what he thought of it.

"I am ashamed to see you engaged in such a business, Benjamin," said he.

"Why so, father?"

"Because it is not an honourable business. You are not a poet, and can write nothing worthy of being printed."

"James approved of the pieces," said Benjamin, "and proposed that I should print and sell them."

"James is not a judge of poetry," replied his father. "It is wretched stuff, and I am ashamed that you are known as the author. Look here, let me show you wherein it is defective;" and here Mr. Franklin began to read it over aloud, and to criticise it. He was a man of sound sense, and competent to expose the faults of such a composition. He proceeded with his criticisms, without sparing the young author's feelings at all, until Benjamin himself began to be sorry that he had undertaken the enterprise.

"There, I want you should promise me," said his father, "that you will never deal in such wares again, and that you will stick to your business of setting up type."

"Perhaps I may improve by practice," said Benjamin, "so that I may yet be able to write something worthy of being read. You couldn't expect me to write very well at first."

"But you are not a poet," continued Mr. Franklin. "It is not in you, and, even if it was, I should not advise you to write it; for poets are generally beggars,—poor, shiftless members of society."

"That is news to me," responded Benjamin. "How does it happen, then, that some of their works are so popular?"

"Because a true poet can write something worthy of being read, while a mere verse-maker, like yourself, writes only doggerel, that is not worth the paper on which it is printed. Now I advise you to let verse-making alone, and attend closely to your business, both for your own sake and your brother's."

Mr. Franklin was rather severe upon Benjamin, although what he said of his verses was true. Still, it was a commendable effort in the boy to try to improve his mind. Some of the best poets who have lived wrote mere doggerel when they began. Many of our best prose-writers, too, were exceedingly faulty writers at first. It is a noble effort of a boy to try to put his thoughts into writing. If he does not succeed in the first instance, by patience, energy, and perseverance he may triumph at last. Benjamin might not have acted wisely in selling his verses about town, but his brother, so much older and more experienced than himself, should bear the censure of that, since it was done by his direction.

The decided opposition that Mr. Franklin showed to verse-making put a damper upon Benjamin's poetical aspirations. The air-castle that his youthful imagination had built, in consequence of the rapid sale of his literary wares, tumbled to ruin at once. He went back to the office and his work quite crest-fallen.

"What has happened now?" inquired James, noticing that Benjamin looked somewhat less smiling.

"Father doesn't think much of my printing and selling verses of my own," replied Benjamin. "He has been giving me a real lecture, so that I am almost ashamed of myself."

"How is that," said James, "does he dislike your pieces?"

"Yes; and he will not allow that they have any merit. He read them over in his way, and counted faults enough to show that there is very little poetry in me. A beggar and a poet mean about the same thing to him."

"He ought to remember that you are young," answered James, "and may improve wonderfully in future. You can't expect to write either prose or poetry well without beginning and trying."

"All the trying in the world can do nothing for me, I should judge from father's talk," added Benjamin, rather seriously.

Perhaps it was a good thing for Benjamin to meet with this obstacle in his path to success. According to his own confession, his vanity was inflated by the sale of his ballads, and he might have been puffed up to his future injury, had not his father thus unceremoniously taken the wind out of his sails. There was little danger now, however. After such a severe handling, he was not likely to overrate his poetical talents. It had the effect also to turn his attention to prose writing, which is more substantial and remunerative than poetry, and in this he became distinguished, as we shall see hereafter.

The practice of writing down one's thoughts, called in our schools "composition," is excellent, and ought not to be so generally neglected by the young as it is. It proved a valuable exercise to Benjamin, even before he became renowned in the service of his country. In several instances, while he was yet a youth, it enabled him to secure business, when otherwise he might have been in extreme want. It gave him the ability to conduct his brother's paper, when only sixteen years of age, at a time when the government of the Province incarcerated James, so that the paper would have been crushed but for the ability of Benjamin. When he first commenced business in Philadelphia, also, it enabled him to produce articles for the "Pennsylvania Gazette," which attracted general notice, and opened the way for his becoming both proprietor and editor of the same. And a little later he was able to write a pamphlet on the "*Nature and Necessity of a Paper Currency*," proposing a measure that was carried through the legislature, because the opponents of it had no writer in their ranks competent to answer it. These are only a few examples of the many advantages he derived from early training himself to write, even before he had passed the dew of his youth. In age he referred to this practice of his boyhood with much pleasure, and regarded it as one of the fortunate exercises that contributed to his eminent success.

Many such facts as the following might be cited upon this subject. A farmer's son began, at fourteen years of age, to write something every day, after his work was done, in a blank-book which he kept for the purpose. He persevered in the practice for several years, and acquired a facility in composition before he thought of having a liberal education. The consequence was, that his friends became earnest to have him educated, and he was sent to college, where he ranked high as a writer; and he is now about entering the ministry, under very flattering circumstances. Few young men have more ease and power of writing at the commencement of their ministerial work; and it all results from his early self-discipline in the exercise of composition.

CHAPTER X.

THE DISPUTE.

BENJAMIN was intimate, at this time, with a youth by the name of John Collins. He was intelligent, sprightly, and fond of books, so that he was a very agreeable companion. They differed somewhat in their opinions upon various subjects, and frequently found themselves engaged in earnest disputation. When other boys were accustomed to spend their time in foolish talking and jesting, Benjamin and John were warmly discussing some question of importance, well suited to improve the mind. One day their conversation related to the education of the sexes.

"It would be a waste of money," said John, "to attempt to educate girls as thoroughly as boys are educated; for the female sex are inferior to the male in intellectual endowment."

"Pshaw!" exclaimed Benjamin; "you know better than that. The girls are not so simple as you think they are. I believe that women are not a whit inferior to men in their mental qualities."

"I should like to know where you discover the evidence of it?" replied John. "There is no proof of it in the works they have written."

"That may be true, and still they stand upon an equality in respect to intellect. For not half so much is done to educate them as there is to educate the male sex. How can you tell whether they are mentally inferior or not, until they are permitted to enjoy equal advantages?"

"As we tell many other things," answered John. "Women do not need so high mental endowments as men, since they are not required to lead off in the different branches of business, or to prosecute the sciences. I can see no wisdom in bestowing talents upon them which they never use, and it is often said that 'nothing is made in vain.'"

"Well, I must go," said Benjamin, "but I think you have a weak cause to defend. If I had the time I could make out a case."

"A poor one, I guess," quickly added John. "We will see, the next time we meet, who can make out a case."

"It will be some time before we meet again," responded Benjamin, "and our ardour will be cooled before that time, I am thinking. But it will do us no harm to discuss the subject."

"If we keep our temper," said John, tacking his sentence to the last word of Benjamin's reply. And so saying, they parted.

After Benjamin had revolved the subject still more in his mind, he became anxious to commit his argument to writing. Accordingly, with pen and paper in hand, he sat down to frame the best argument he could in favour of educating the female sex. He wrote it in the form of a letter, addressed to his friend Collins, and, after having completed, he copied it in a fair hand, and sent it to him. This brought back a long reply, which made it necessary for Benjamin to pen an answer. In this way the correspondence continued, until several letters had passed between them, and each one had gained the victory in his own estimation.

One day Benjamin's father met with these letters accidentally, and he read them over, and was somewhat impressed with their character.

"What are these, Benjamin," he inquired, at the same time holding up the letters.

Benjamin smiled, and rather hesitated to reply.

"So it seems you have been engaged in a controversy with John," continued Mr. Franklin. "You have both done very well, though I think there is some chance of improvement yet."

"Have you read them all?" inquired Benjamin.

"I have, and must say that, in some respects, John has the advantage of you."

"In what has he the advantage?" asked Benjamin, with some anxiety.

"Well, John writes in a more finished style than you do," answered Mr. Franklin. "His expressions are more elegant, and there is more method and perspicuity in his composition."

"I rather think you are prejudiced," said Benjamin, with a smile.

"*I* rather think not," answered his father. "You have the advantage of John in correct spelling, and in pointing your sentences, which is the consequence of working in the printing-office. But I can convince you that less method and clearness characterize your letters than his."

"I am ready to be convinced," added Benjamin. "I hardly expect I have attained perfection in writing yet."

His father then proceeded to read from the letters of each, with the design of showing that John's writing was more perspicuous, and that there was more method in his argument. Nor was it a very difficult task.

"I am convinced," said Benjamin, before his father had read all he intended to read. "I can make improvement in those points without much trouble. There is certainly a good chance for it."

"That is what I want you should see," rejoined his father, "I am really pleased with your letters, for they show me that you have talents to improve. My only object in calling your attention to these defects is to aid you in cultivating your mental powers."

This kind, paternal criticism was a very happy thing for Benjamin. It had the effect to make him more careful in his compositions, and to beget within him both a desire and resolve to improve. Not long after, he met with an old volume of the Spectator, in a bookstore; and knowing that it would be a good model by which to form the style, he determined to purchase it. He bought it at a low price, and began to study it with reference to improving the style of his composition. The method which he adopted to discipline himself, by the aid of this work, is proof of his patience, perseverance, and desire to excel. In the first place, he read it over and over, until he became very well acquainted with its contents. Then he took some of the papers it contained, and made short hints of the sentiments of each sentence, and laid them by for a few days; and then, without referring to the book, he proceeded to put those thoughts into sentences, and thus went through each paper,—a long and laborious work. When he had completed a paper in this way, he carefully compared his Spectator with the original, and was able thereby to discover and correct many errors in his style. He found that he was very deficient in the command of language.

"If you had not discouraged me in writing poetry," said he to his father, "I should have found it of much service now."

"How so?" inquired Mr. Franklin.

"If I had continued to write poetry, I should have been obliged to select words that would rhyme, and this would have made me familiar with a larger number of words, and the choicest ones too. I am greatly troubled now to find words to express my thoughts."

"I should have had no objections to your writing poetry with such an object in view; but to print and sell it about town was carrying the thing a little too far," replied Mr. Franklin. "It is not too late to begin now. I rather think you have discovered an important defect in your writing. John evidently has a better command of language than you have, hence his style is more polished. But you are at work, now, in the right way to improve. Perseverance will accomplish the thing."

"I am going to do this," said Benjamin; "I shall take some of the tales in the book and put them into verse, and then, after a while, change them back again."

"That will be a good exercise," answered his father, much pleased with his son's desire to improve. "If your patience holds out, you will be amply rewarded, in the end, for all your labour."

This last purpose, Benjamin executed with much zeal, and thus divided his time between putting tales into poetry, and then turning them into prose. He also jumbled his collection of hints into confusion, and so let them lie for some weeks, when he would again reduce them to order, and write out the sentences to the end of the subject.

For a printer-boy to accomplish so much, when he must work through the day in the office, seemed hardly possible. But, at this period, Benjamin allowed no moments to run to waste. He always kept a book by him in the office, and every spare moment was employed over its pages. In the morning, before he went to work, he found some time for reading and study. He was an early riser, not, perhaps, because he had no inclination to lie in bed, but because he had more to improve his mind. He gained time enough in the morning, by this early rising, to acquire more knowledge than some youths and young men do by constantly going to school. In the evening, he found still more time for mental improvement, extending his studies often far into the night. It was his opinion that people generally consume more time than is necessary in sleep, and one of his maxims, penned in early manhood, was founded on that opinion. The maxim is, "The sleeping fox catches no poultry."

It is not strange that a boy who subjected himself to such close discipline for a series of years should write some of the best maxims upon this subject when he became a man. Take the following, in addition to those cited in a former chapter:—

"There are no gains without pains; then help hands, for I have no lands."

"Industry pays debts, while despair increaseth them."

"Never leave that till to-morrow which you can do to-day."

"Leisure is time for doing something useful."

"A life of leisure and a life of laziness are two things."

"Fly pleasures, and they will follow you. The diligent spinner has a large shift, and, now I have a sheep and a cow, every one bids me good-morrow."

"Be ashamed to catch yourself idle."

"Handle your tools without mittens; remember that the cat in gloves catches no mice."

"There is much to be done, and perhaps you are weak-handed: but stick to it steadily, and you will see great effects, for constant dropping wears away stones; and by diligence and patience the mouse ate in two the cable; and little strokes fell great oaks."

"Early to bed, and early to riseMakes a man healthy, wealthy, and wise."

Here is the genuine gold of thought,—whole volumes of counsel worked down into single flashing lines of truth,—just such utterances as we might expect from the lips of one who was early taught to walk in the ways of wisdom. All along in the future of Benjamin's life, we shall see these maxims illustrated, proving that they are living and bright realities.

In order to prosecute his purposes, Benjamin took a step, at this period, for which he censured himself long after. Being away from his father's house, in a boarding-place provided by his brother, he violated the Sabbath day by devoting its sacred hours to mental improvement. At home, his parents had ever required that he should attend public worship; but now he neglected the house of God, that he might command the more time for study. It was a grave breach of a divine commandment, and a disregard of parental authority, which he afterwards deeply regretted. At the time, he was obliged to hold long parleys with conscience, which told him that he ought still to visit the sanctuary, and devote Sabbath hours to sacred duties. Yet his great thirst for knowledge overcame his regard for holy time.

It must appear quite evident to the reader by this time, that Benjamin derived much benefit from his conversation with John Collins upon a useful topic. A large majority of boys, of their age, spend their leisure moments in vain and useless talking. They think not of self-improvement, and scarcely desire to be benefited in this way. The most unmeaning and thoughtless words escape from their lips, and a sound, sensible, valuable conversation they seldom, if ever, attempt. What an excellent example is that of young Franklin and Collins, discussing a question of importance, instead of wasting their breath in meaningless chatter! It stimulated the former to consult the best models of style in composition, and was the real occasion of his adopting a most critical and thorough plan of self-culture. All this the consequence of conversing properly, instead of spending leisure moments in boyish antics, or uttering nonsense!

The reader need not infer that violation of the Sabbath, and disregard of parental counsels, are less heinous sins than some would grant, since Benjamin was guilty of both, and yet he did not go to ruin. For ten boys who do the same things that he did are ruined thereby, where one is saved. The father of Walter Scott forbade his reading fictitious works, yet he concealed them in a sly place, and read them when his father's eye was not upon him; and they served to stimulate his mind to pursue a most brilliant literary career. In like manner, Pope, the distinguished poet, strolled into the theatre in his boyhood, when he was away from his parents at school, and there the first aspiration of his soul for that sphere of mental effort in which he became distinguished, was begotten. But these examples cannot be cited in favour of novel-reading and theatre-going; for they are exceptions to a general rule. The great mass of the youth who allow themselves to be fascinated by the novel and theatre make shipwreck of their hopes.

CHAPTER XI.

PLAIN FARE.

"How much will you allow me a week if I will board myself?" inquired Benjamin of James. "It costs you now more than you need to pay." James was still boarding Benjamin in a family near by, being himself yet unmarried.

"Then you think I am paying more a week for your board than it is worth?" replied his brother.

"No more than you will be obliged to pay in any other family, but more than I shall ask you," answered Benjamin.

"Then you think of opening a boarding-house for the special accommodation of Benjamin Franklin?" which was treating his request rather lightly.

"I propose to board myself," said Benjamin. "I do not eat meat of any kind, as you know, so that I can do it very easily, and I will agree to do it, if you will pay me half the money weekly which you pay for my board."

"Agreed," replied James. "The bargain is made. When will you begin?"

"To-morrow," was Benjamin's laconic reply.

Benjamin had been reading a work on "vegetable diet," by one Tryon, and it was this which induced him to discard meat as an article of food. Mr. Tryon, in his work, gave directions for cooking vegetables, and such dishes as a vegetarian might use, so that the matter of boarding was made quite simple. Benjamin really thought that this mode of living was best for health and strength, though his chief object in proposing to board himself was to obtain money to purchase books. He had been trying a vegetable diet for some time in the family where he and his brother had boarded, and had often been both ridiculed and censured for his oddity. Perhaps he wanted to get away where he could eat as he pleased, with no one to say, "Why do ye so?" But most of all he wanted to command more money, that he might gratify his thirst for knowledge.

James was very willing to accept the proposition, as it would bring a little more money into his pocket. He was an avaricious and penurious young man, who thought mainly of making money in his business, and it was of little consequence to him whether he made it out of his brother or some one else.

"How much do you make by boarding yourself, Ben?" inquired James, some weeks after the experiment was commenced.

"I save just half of the money you pay me," answered Benjamin, "so that it costs me just one quarter as much as you paid for my board."

"You understand economy, I must confess," said his brother. "However, I have no fault to find if you are satisfied."

"The money I save is not the best part of it," continued Benjamin. "I save about a half-hour every noon for reading. After I have eaten my meal, I usually read as long as that before you return from dinner."

"Not a very sumptuous meal I reckon," said James dryly; "sawdust-pudding, perhaps, with cold-water sauce!"

"Nothing so difficult to procure as that," responded Benjamin. "A biscuit or a slice of bread, with a tart or a few raisins, and a glass of water, make a good dinner for me; and then my head is all the lighter for study."

"I should think you might have a light head with such living," added James, "and your body will be as light before many weeks I prophesy."

"I will risk it. I am on a study now that requires a clear head, and I am determined to master it."

"What is that?"

"It is Cocker's Arithmetic."

"Begin to wish you knew something about arithmetic by this time," added James sarcastically. "Making up for misspent time, I see!" Here was a fling at Benjamin's dislike of arithmetic when he was sent to school. We have seen that he accomplished nothing in figures, either at the public school or when he was under Mr. Brownwell's tuition. Liking some other studies better, he neglected this, and now, as is generally the case, he regretted his error, and applied himself to acquire that which he might have acquired before. It was a difficult task for him, but his patience and perseverance, together with his economy of time, and temperance in eating and drinking, enabled him to accomplish his object. Then he read a work on Navigation, and made himself particularly familiar with the geometry which it contained. "Locke on the Understanding," and "The Art of Thinking," were two other works that he read closely while he was living on a vegetable diet. All these works were difficult to be mastered by a boy not yet fourteen years of age. Yet he was not discouraged by this fact; it rather seemed to arouse him to greater efforts.

"You calculate time as closely as a miser does his money, Ben," said James.

"As little as I have for myself requires that I should calculate closely," was his reply. "Time is money to you, or else you would allow me a little more to myself; and it is more than money to me."

"How so?" inquired James.

"It enables me to acquire knowledge, which I cannot buy with money. Unless I was saving of my time, I should not be able to read or study at all, having to work so constantly."

Perhaps, at this time, Benjamin laid the foundation for that economy which distinguished him in later life, and about which he often wrote. Among his wise sayings touching this subject are the following:—

"If you would be wealthy, think of saving, as well as of getting."

"What maintains one vice would bring up two children."

"Many a little makes a mickle."

"A small leak will sink a ship."

"At a great pennyworth pause awhile."

"Silks and satins, scarlet and velvets, put out the kitchen fire."

"Always taking out of the meal-tub, and never putting in, soon comes to the bottom."

"For age and want save while you may,—No morning sun lasts a whole day."

"It is easier to build two chimneys than to keep one in fuel."

"A penny saved is a penny earned."

"A penny saved is twopence clear; A pin a day is a groat a year."

"He that wastes idly a groat's worth of his time per day, one day with another, wastes the privilege of using one hundred pounds each day."

To a young tradesman he wrote, in the year 1748:—

> "Remember that time is money. He that can earn ten shilling a day by his labour, and goes abroad or sits idle one half that day, though he spend but sixpence during his diversion or idleness, ought not to reckon that the only expense; he has really spent, or rather thrown away, five shillings besides....

"In short, the way to wealth, if you desire it, is as plain as the way to market. It depends chiefly on two words, *industry* and *frugality*; that is, waste neither *time* nor *money*, but make the best use of both. Without industry and frugality nothing will do, and with them everything. He that gets all he can honestly, and saves all he gets (necessary expenses excepted), will certainly become *rich*,—if that Being who governs the world, to whom all should look for a blessing on their honest endeavours, doth not, in his wise providence, otherwise determine."

In these excellent sayings, time and money are spoken of together, because time is money; and Franklin was never more economical of one than of the other. All that he says of frugality in respect to property applies equally to time, and *vice versâ*. In his boyhood, when he adopted a vegetable diet, he had no money to save, so that the most of his economy related to time. It being to him as valuable as gold, he was prompted to husband it as well. To some observers he might have appeared to be penurious, but those who knew him saw that he reduced another of his own maxims to practice: "We must save, that we may share." He never sought to save time or money that he might hoard the more of worldly goods to enjoy in a selfish way. He was ever generous and liberal, as we shall see hereafter. The superficial observer might suppose that a niggardly spirit prompted him to board himself,—that he adopted a vegetable diet for the sake of mere lucre. But nothing could be wider from the truth than such a view. We cannot discover the least desire to *hoard* the money he saved. He laid it out in books, and such things as aided him in self-improvement. He believed in temperate eating, as we have already said, and the following maxims of his show the same thing:—

"Who dainties love, shall beggars prove."

"Fools make feasts, and wise men eat them."

"Buy what thou hast no need of, and ere long thou shalt sell thy necessaries."

He saw that he could never possess the books he needed, or command the time, if his appetite for luxuries was gratified. In his circumstances, the most marked self-denial was necessary, to gain his object. At the same time, he believed it would make him more healthy to be abstemious. There was not an iota of stinginess in his habitual economy.

Economy of time or money is praiseworthy only when it is done to command the means of being useful,—which was true of Franklin. When it is practised to gratify a sordid love of money, it is ignoble and sinful.

About this time, Benjamin and John Collins had another interview,—differing somewhat from the one already described, as the following dialogue will show:—

"What book is this, Ben?" inquired John, taking up one from the table.

"It is an old English Grammar which I came across the other day," answered Benjamin. "It has two chapters, near the close, on Rhetoric and Logic, that are valuable."

"Valuable to you, perhaps, but not to me," said John. "What shall I ever want of Rhetoric or Logic?"

"Everybody ought to know something about them," answered Benjamin. "They have already helped me, in connection with the works of Shaftesbury, to understand some things about religion better. I have believed some doctrines just because my parents taught me so."

"Then you do not believe all that you have been taught about religion, if I understand you?"

"No, I am free to say that I do not. There is neither reason nor wisdom in portions of the creed of the Church."

"Why, Ben, you surprise me. You are getting to be quite infidel for a boy. It won't do for you to read Logic and Shaftesbury any more, if you are so easily upset by them."

"Made to understand better by them what is right and what is wrong," answered Benjamin. "The fact is, very few persons think for themselves. They are religious because they are so instructed. They embrace the religion of their parents without asking themselves what is true or false."

"There is not much danger that you will do that," said John. "Present appearances rather indicate that the religious opinions of your father will be blown sky-high,"—though John did not mean quite so much as his language denotes.

"You do not understand me. I respect my parents and their religious opinions, though I doubt some of the doctrines they have taught, and which I never carefully examined until recently."

"I must go," said John; "at another time, I will hear more;"—and he hurried away to his business, which was waiting for him.

Benjamin had read carefully the works of Collins and Shaftesbury, which were well suited to unsettle his religious belief. At the time of this interview, he was really a doubter, though not avowedly opposed to religion. The fact shows the necessity of using care in selecting books to be read, and the danger of tampering with those that speak lightly of the Gospel. Even a mind as strong as that of Benjamin was warped by the sophistries of such a book, and it was some years before he recovered wholly from the sad effects of such reading. His early religious culture, however, and his disposition and ability to perceive the truth, finally saved him from the abyss of infidelity, as will appear more evident in the pages that follow.

CHAPTER XII.

THE NEWSPAPER.

ON the seventeenth day of January, 1721, James Franklin began to issue a newspaper, called "THE NEW ENGLAND COURANT." It was the third one at the time in the whole country. The first paper—"THE BOSTON NEWSLETTER"—was established in 1704, two years before the birth of Benjamin. It was only a half-sheet of paper, about the size of an eight by twelve inch pane of glass, "in two pages folio, with two columns on each page." Consequently, it could not have contained more printed matter than is now compressed into half a page of one of the Boston dailies. Yet it was considered a very important undertaking for the times.

When James Franklin proposed to start the third paper in America, some of his friends thought it was a wild project, and endeavoured to dissuade him from it. They saw nothing but ruin before him, and used every persuasion to lead him to abandon the enterprise. They thought that two newspapers, such as would now excite a smile by their inferior size, were quite enough for the country. Take this fact, in connection with the present abundance of papers, and the contrast presents a striking view of the progress of America since that day. At that time there was not a daily paper in the land. Now there are eight in the city of Boston alone, having an aggregate daily circulation of about *one hundred and twenty-five thousand*, which would amount to nearly FORTY MILLION sheets in a year,—more than enough to furnish every man, woman, and child in the country with one sheet each. All this from the daily press of Boston, where, one hundred and forty years ago, it was thought that a third weekly newspaper, scarcely large enough to wrap a baker's loaf in, could not be supported! Bind them into volumes, containing one hundred sheets each, and we have an enormous library of daily newspapers, numbering *four hundred thousand volumes*, the annual production of the Boston daily press in 1860! And this only the aggregate of eight different papers, while Boston alone now has *one hundred and forty* papers and periodicals of all sorts, and the State of Massachusetts nearly *three hundred!* How marvellous the change since Franklin was a poor printer-boy!

But look at these eight daily papers of Boston again. Suppose they measure a yard each in width, upon an average, when opened;—here we have one hundred and twenty-five thousand yards of newspapers emanating daily from only eight presses of Franklin's native city; which is equal to *seventy-one miles* per day, and *four hundred and twenty-six* miles per week, and *twenty-two thousand one hundred and fifty-two* miles in a year! This is truly surprising. Almost paper enough from the eight daily presses of Boston alone, every year, to reach around the earth!

Or, suppose we weigh these papers. If ten of them weigh a single pound, then each day's issue weighs *twelve thousand five hundred pounds*, each week's issue amounts to *seventy-five thousand pounds*, which swells the annual aggregate to about *four million pounds*. Load this yearly production upon waggons, one ton on each, and we have *two thousand and two horse loads of newspapers* from these eight presses in a year! Again, we say, how marvellous the change!

If eight daily papers of Boston throw off this vast amount of reading-matter in a year, what immense quantities are supplied by all the presses in the land! Could the actual statistics be laid before us in round numbers, doubtless the most credulous even would be amazed at the result.

But to return. James decided to issue his paper, notwithstanding the advice of some of his friends to the contrary, and he thus opened the subject to Benjamin:—

"I have resolved to issue a paper, and it will require our united exertions to make it go. No doubt I shall meet with opposition, and perhaps shall fail in the attempt, but I have determined to fail *trying*."

"What particular service can I render?" inquired Benjamin.

"Aside from your usual work of type-setting, you are qualified to look after the composition and spelling of the articles in each number, and a part of your work shall be to deliver the paper to subscribers from week to week."

"And be collector, too, I suppose," added Benjamin, rather fancying the idea of issuing a paper from the office.

"As you like about that," answered his brother, "though it may be convenient, often, to have you render such a service."

"I suppose you don't mean to make me editor also?" he added, rather jestingly; probably not dreaming that he should ever conduct the publication.

"I think not at present," was his brother's reply. "Printer, news-carrier, and collector, will be as much honour as you can withstand at once;" and he had as little idea of the part Benjamin would play in the work as the boy had himself.

Accordingly the paper was issued at the appointed time, creating quite a stir in the community, and provoking remarks *pro* and *con* concerning its appearance, character, and prospects. Agreeably to the arrangement,

Benjamin delivered the numbers to subscribers, and perhaps he sold the paper about the streets, thus acting as one of the first newsboys on this western continent.

Among the friends of James Franklin, and the patrons of his paper, were several men who possessed considerable talent for writing, and they were accustomed to assemble at the printing-office, and discuss questions connected with the circulation of the paper. Benjamin's ears were usually open to their conversation,—and he heard the merits of different articles set forth, and learned that certain ones were quite popular, and elicited favourable remarks from readers generally. This excited his ambition, and he earnestly desired to try his own ability in writing for the paper. He feared, however, that his composition would not be regarded favourably, if it were known who was the author; so he hit upon this expedient. He resolved to write an anonymous article, in his very best style, and get it into his brother's hand so as not to awaken his suspicion. Accordingly, the article was prepared, and at night it was tucked under the printing-office door, where James found it in the morning. As usual, several of his writers came in about their usual time, and Benjamin had the happiness of hearing the following discussion:—

"Here is a good article, that I found under the door this morning," said James, at the same time holding it up.

"Who is the author of it?" inquired one.

"It is anonymous," replied James, "and I have not the least idea who wrote it."

"What is the subject?" asked another; and the subject was announced.

"Let us hear it read," proposed a third. "You read it aloud to us, James." So James proceeded to read the article aloud, while all listened with deep interest. All the while Benjamin was busily employed at his work, though his ears were never more willing to hear. You may be sure that he felt rather queerly while his composition was undergoing this test, and a close observer might have observed a sly, comical twinkle of his eye. The reading went on without one of the company dreaming that the author stood at their elbow.

"Capital!" exclaimed one, as the last line was read. "Who can the author be?"

"As a general thing," said James, "I shall not insert articles from persons unknown to me, but this is so good that I shall publish it."

"By all means," said one of the company. "We shall soon find out the author; it is a difficult matter to keep such things secret for a long time."

"The author is evidently a person of ability," added another; "every sentence in that article is charged with thought. I should judge that he wanted only culture to make him a writer of the first class."

"Publishing the article will be as likely as anything to bring out the author," said James.

It was decided to print the article, all having approved of the same, much to the satisfaction of Benjamin, who awaited the decision with some anxiety. Now he scarcely knew how to act in regard to the piece, whether to father it at once, or still conceal its parentage. On the whole, however, he decided to withhold its authorship for the present, and try his hand again in the same way. Much encouraged by the success of his first effort, Benjamin was prepared to produce even a better article on the second trial, which was discussed and approved in the same way as the first. Thus he wrote, and put under the door at night, a number of articles, all of which were pronounced good by James and his friends. It was a time of much interest and excitement to Benjamin, since he was the "unknown character" so much extolled by the patrons of the "Courant." To hear his own articles remarked upon and praised, when no one dreamed that a boy like himself could be the author, was well suited to stir up his feelings, if not to inflate his vanity. Many persons in like circumstances would be allured into indiscretions and improprieties. But Benjamin wisely kept his own secrets, while he industriously continued to set up types, fearing that disclosure at the present time might knock all his plans into "pie."

There is no doubt that this was one of the incidents of Benjamin's boyhood that decided his future eminent career. It was a good thing to bring out his talents as a writer thus early, and it evidently fostered his love of an exercise that was of the first importance in the improvement of his mind. From the time that he wrote the first article which he put under the door of the printing-office, he did not cease to write more or less for the public eye. He had written before, as we have seen, but his father had rather put a damper on his composing for the public to read, and, besides, the newspaper was a channel of communicating with readers altogether new to him. It was well suited to awaken deep interest in his heart, and to incite him to put forth his noblest efforts.

The great English statesman, CANNING, was sent to school at Eton, at twelve years of age, where he originated a mimic House of Commons among his schoolmates. Here they established a boy periodical, called the "Microcosm." It was a weekly publication, and issued from Windsor. It was conducted "after the plan of the 'Spectator,' the design being to treat the characteristics of the boys at Eton as Addison and his friends had done those of general society." In this paper several members of the school figured with credit to themselves, though no one was more earnest to sustain it than young Canning. It became one of the prominent influences that decided his future course, bringing out his talents, and stimulating his mind to labour in this honourable way. It also exerted a decided influence upon the character of another boy, named Frere, who afterwards shone as a writer in the pages of the "Anti-Jacobin."

At the present day, in many seminaries and village lyceums, several literary enterprises are sustained, to the no small advantage of the young who become personally interested in it. Every youth who desires to cultivate his mental faculties ought to hail such enterprises with joy, and pledge his noblest efforts to sustain them. It may be that it is discouragingly difficult for him to write at first; but let him persevere, with patience and firm resolve, and he will prove to himself that "practice makes perfect." There is no better exercise for his mind than this, and none better adapted to inspire him with a dauntless resolve to acquire knowledge.

The Mysterious Contributor.—See page 123.

CHAPTER XIII.

THE CAT OUT OF THE BAG.

BENJAMIN was so highly gratified with the favourable remarks he heard about his articles, and especially that different persons, in guessing who the author might be, usually guessed some writer of distinction, that he could keep the secret no longer. He was eager to make the fact known, that the much talked of essays emanated from his own pen; and soon "the cat was let out of the bag."

Having a good opportunity, in reply to some remark of James about "the last article found under the door," he said, "I know who the author is."

"You know?" exclaimed James with surprise. "Why have you not disclosed it before?"

"Because I thought it was not wise. It is not best to tell all we know always."

"But you have heard us discuss this matter over and over, and take measures to discover the author, and yet you have never intimated that you knew anything about it."

"Well, the author did not wish to be known, until the right time came, and that is a good reason for keeping the matter secret, I think."

"Will you tell me who the author is now?" asked James, impatient to obtain the long-sought information.

"Perhaps I will, if you are very anxious to know."

"You know that I am. Who is it?"

"It is Benjamin Franklin."

"What!" exclaimed James, astonished almost beyond measure by the disclosure; "do you mean to say that you wrote those articles?"

"Certainly I do."

"But it is not your handwriting."

"I disguised my hand in order to conceal the authorship."

"What could possibly be your object in doing so?"

"That the articles might be fairly examined. If I had proposed to write an article for your paper, you would have said that I, a printer-boy, could write nothing worthy of print."

Here the conversation dropped, and James appeared to be abstracted in thought. He said but little about the matter to Benjamin, neither commending nor censuring, until his literary friends came in again.

"I have discovered the author of those articles," said James.

"You have? who can it be?" one asked.

"No one that you have dreamed of," answered James.

"Do tell us who it is, and put an end to our anxiety," said one of the number, who could hardly wait for the desired information.

"There he is," replied James, pointing to Benjamin, who was setting up types a little more briskly than usual. The whole company were amazed.

"Can it be?" cried out one; "you are joking."

Now Benjamin had to speak for himself; for they all turned to him with their inquiries, as if they thought there must be some mistake or deception about the matter. But he found little difficulty in convincing them that he was the real author of the pieces; whereupon they commended him in a manner that was rather perilous to one who had the smallest share of pride in his heart.

From that time Benjamin was a favourite with the literary visitors at the office. They showed him much more attention than they did James, and said so much in his praise, as a youth of unusual promise, that James became jealous and irritable. He was naturally passionate and tyrannical, and this sudden and unexpected exaltation of Benjamin developed his overbearing spirit. He began to find fault seriously and unreasonably with him, and a disposition to oppress him was soon apparent. He went so far as to beat him severely with a rod, on several occasions, reconciling the matter with his conscience by saying that he was master, and Benjamin was his apprentice. His whole conduct towards his younger brother was unjust and cruel, and the latter became restive and discontented under it. He made known his grievances to his father, who censured James for his conduct, and took the part of Benjamin. But the best efforts of his father to reconcile matters proved abortive, because James's manifest opposition was so aroused against his brother, on account of his sudden rise to comparative distinction. Other causes might have operated to awaken James's hostility, but this was evidently a prominent one.

Benjamin was so dissatisfied with his treatment that he resolved to leave his brother as soon as possible. He was indentured to him, as we have seen, so that it was difficult for him to get away. Being bound to him until he became twenty-one years of age, the law held him firmly there, notwithstanding the injustice he experienced. Still, for the present, he laboured on in the office, and the paper continued to be issued.

We are reminded that the printing-office has furnished many eminent scholars to the world. Young men have there come in contact with printed matter that has aroused their intellects to action, and caused them to press onward, with new resolves, in paths of usefulness and renown.

In the case of Benjamin, the circumstance of his connection with the office just at the time a new paper was established called out a certain kind of talent he possessed, and thus helped to make him what he became. Success depends in a great measure in early directing the young in the path to which their natural endowments point. Thus Lord Nelson, who distinguished himself in the service of his country, was early placed in just those circumstances that appealed to his fortitude and other heroic attributes. That he possessed by nature remarkable courage and determination, in connection with other qualities that usually accompany these, is evident from an incident of his childhood. One day he strayed from home with a cow-boy in search of birds' nests, and being missed at dinner-time, and inquiries made for him, the startling suspicion was awakened that he had been carried off by gipsies. The alarm of his parents was great, and a careful search was instituted, when he was found sitting on the banks of a stream which he could not cross, unconcerned and happy.

"I wonder, child," said his grandmother, when he was brought back in safety to the family, "that hunger and fear did not drive you home."

"Fear!" exclaimed the heroic lad, "I never saw fear,—what is it?"

He was taken by his uncle into the naval service while he was yet a boy, where the scenes of every day were suited to develop and strengthen the heroic qualities of his nature. He became known to the world, not merely for his victories at Trafalgar and on the Nile, but for other essential service rendered to his native land.

The same was true of Buxton, Wilberforce, Pascal, Handel, Canova, Dr. Chalmers, and many others. Providence opened before them the path to which their native qualities directed.

We have spoken of the advantage of occasionally writing compositions, as Benjamin was wont to write, and another fact illustrating this point has just come to our notice. It is an incident belonging to the history of the Boston Young Men's Temperance Society. In addition to its being a temperance organization, it was sustained for mutual mental improvement. With other exercises, the members read lectures of their own preparing at the meetings,—a very important and valuable arrangement. One evening a member delivered a lecture upon the character and objects of the society, which was listened to by a young man who dropped into the hall for the first time. He was so well pleased with the design of the association, as set forth in the lecture, that he joined it at the close of the exercises. He began at once to fulfil the requirements of the society in writing compositions, and they were so well written that the author of the aforesaid lecture said to him one evening—

"Why do you not write something for the press? If I possessed your ability I should do it."

The young man received the compliment with becoming modesty, expressing some lack of confidence in his abilities; but it set him to thinking. The result was that he prepared a short article for a Boston paper, which was accepted; and the way was thereby opened to his becoming a constant contributor to its columns. The end is not yet, though he is now the author of the popular "Optic Library." Thus so small a matter as writing a brief article for a newspaper may herald a career of literary fame.

CHAPTER XIV.

THE ARREST.

"HAVE you heard what they are doing in the Assembly?" asked Benjamin one afternoon, as he entered the office under considerable excitement, addressing his inquiry to James.

"Doing?" answered James; "doing their business, I suppose;"—a reply that did not indicate precisely his knowledge of the legislative doings, since he had heard of the business before them, and was somewhat troubled by it.

"They are certainly going to arrest you for libel, and I heard a gentleman say, in the street, that they would show you no favour;" and Benjamin made this revelation with considerable warmth of feeling. The idea of his brother's arrest and imprisonment excited him in no small degree.

On the same day the following order was passed in the General Court:—

"IN COUNCIL, Jan. 14, 1722.

"Whereas the paper, called the New England Courant, of this day's date, contains many passages in which the Holy Scriptures are perverted, and the Civil Government, Ministers, and People of this Province highly reflected on,

Ordered, That William Tailer, Samuel Sewell, and Penn Townsend, Esqrs., with such as the Honourable House of Representatives shall join, be a committee to consider and report what is proper for the Court to do thereon."

The House of Representatives concurred, and the committee reported:—

"That James Franklin, the printer and publisher thereof (the Courant), be strictly forbidden by this Court to print or publish the New England Courant, or any other pamphlet or paper of the like nature, except it be first supervised by the Secretary of this Province; and the Justices of his Majesty's Sessions of the Peace for the County of Suffolk, at their next adjournment, be directed to take sufficient bonds of the said Franklin for twelve months' time."

The result was, that James was arrested and confined four weeks in the "stone gaol," from which he was released by his voluntary pledge to regard the honour of the Court. Benjamin was arrested, also; but was discharged on the ground that he acted as an apprentice, and was obliged to do the bidding of his master.

It appears that there was considerable dissatisfaction in the Province with the British government, under which the people lived. The Courant espoused the cause of the dissatisfied party, and, perhaps unwisely, attacked the government and its officers, together with the ministers of the Gospel, whose sympathies seemed to be with the dominant party. It was a time of considerable excitement, so that a little firebrand thrown into the community was sure to make a great fire. But the immediate cause of his arrest was the appearance of the following article in his paper, which was a slur upon the government for tardiness in fitting out a ship to cruise after a pirate seen off Block Island. The article purported to be written by a correspondent in Newport, R. I., and read thus:—

> "We are advised from Boston, that the government of the Massachusetts are fitting out a ship to go after the pirates, to be commanded by Captain Peter Papillon, and *'tis thought he will sail some time this month, wind and weather permitting.*"

This well-pointed censure, in connection with the many flings and attacks that had preceded it, aroused the General Court to act in their defence without delay.

The club under whose auspices the Courant was conducted, assembled at the office as soon as they knew the decision of the Court, to consider what should be done.

"It is certain," said one, "that you cannot continue to issue the paper against the action of the Court."

"Not in his own name," suggested another. "It may still be published in the name of another person, and thus the legislative order will be evaded."

"How will it do to issue it in Benjamin's name?" inquired James.

"That cannot be done, for he is only an apprentice, as could be very readily proved," was the reply.

"I can easily meet that difficulty," answered James, who was usually ready for a shrewd evasion in such a case.

"Pray, tell us how," asked one of the number, who was disposed to think that the days of the Courant were numbered. "By changing the name?"

"No, I would not change the name. I will return his indenture, with his discharge upon the back of it, and he can show it in case of necessity. We can understand the matter between us, while he will be his own man whenever any trouble may arise about his apprenticeship."

All agreed that this plan would work well, and it was accordingly adopted.

"Benjamin Franklin, publisher and proprietor," said one of the club, rising from his seat and patting Benjamin on the shoulder. "What do you think of that, my son? Rather a young fellow to undertake such an enterprise, but a match, I guess, for the General Court of the Province."

Benjamin was quite unprepared to reply to the merriment of the club on the occasion over his unexpected introduction to an office of which he did not dream in the morning. He was now to appear before the public in quite another relation than that of apprentice,—probably the youngest conductor of a newspaper who ever lived, for he was only sixteen years of age.

Henceforth the paper appeared in the name of Benjamin Franklin, occasioning, by all the circumstances, no little excitement in the town.

James was conveyed to prison, and during his confinement, Benjamin had the whole management of the paper, in which he took occasion to speak very plainly and boldly against the government. Notwithstanding the difficulty that existed between him and his brother, his heart was stirred with resentment against the Court for sending him to jail, and he espoused his cause with as much sympathy and good-will, apparently, as he could have done if no difference had disturbed their intercourse. This was honourable in Benjamin, and showed that he possessed a true brother's heart. For three years the paper was published in his name, although he did not remain with James so long.

We have referred to the time of Benjamin's boyhood as a period of public excitement and disturbance. Great alarm was frequently occasioned, for some time before and some time after his birth, by the depredations of the Indians. The French were hostile to Great Britain; so they sought to stir up, and ally themselves with, the savages, in making inroads upon the Colonies. The consequence was, "wars and rumours of wars," with actual massacres and bloodshed. Benjamin's ears, in his early life, were often saluted with the harrowing tales of slaughter and conflagration, an experience that may have qualified him, in a measure, to act the prominent part he did in achieving the independence of his country, half a century thereafter. Rev. Dr. Willard, who baptized him, was driven from the town of Groton by the Indians in 1675. Later still, only three years before the birth of Benjamin, the town of Deerfield was attacked and burned by these savage tribes, instigated and led on by the French,—and "upwards of forty persons were slain, and more than a hundred were made prisoners." "When the sun was an hour high, the work was finished, and the enemy took their departure, leaving the snow reddened with blood, and the deserted village enveloped in flames." Only two or three years after his birth, the famous attack upon Haverhill was made, when the Indians massacred men, women, and children indiscriminately, a few only escaping their terrible vengeance. The stories of such dreadful cruelties and sufferings were fresh in Benjamin's boyhood, and their effect upon the youthful mind was heightened by the frequent reports of outbreaks and anticipated Indian attacks from different quarters. Thus born and reared in troublous times, our hero was prepared to work out his destiny in the most perilous period of American history.

A single item published in the Courant about this time, will show the young reader that Boston and its environs of that early day did not much resemble the same city now. The item is the following:—

> "It is thought that not less than twenty bears have been killed in about a week's time within two miles of Boston. Two have been killed below the Castle, as they were swimming from one island to another, and one attempted to board a boat out in the bay, but the men defended themselves so well with the boat-hook and oars, that they put out her eyes, and then killed her. On Tuesday last two were killed at Dorchester, one of which weighed sixty pounds a quarter. We hear from Providence that the bears appear to be very thick in those parts."

CHAPTER XV.

THE RUNAWAY.

NOT long after James was released from prison, a fresh difficulty arose between Benjamin and himself. In the quarrel they seemed to forget that they were brothers, who ought to be united by strong ties of affection. James continued to be passionate and domineering, treating his brother with harshness, sometimes even beating him, notwithstanding he was the nominal publisher and editor of a paper. Benjamin thought he was too old to be treated thus—whipped like a little boy—and the result was that he asserted his freedom.

"I am my own man from this time," he cried, holding up his indenture which his brother returned to him, as we saw in a former chapter, in order to evade the officers of justice. "These papers make me free, and I shall take advantage of them to leave you," and he fairly shook them in James's face.

"You know that I never gave them up because I relinquished the bargain we had made," said James. "If you use them to assert your freedom, you will be guilty of a base act."

"I *shall* so use the papers," replied Benjamin defiantly. "I have borne such treatment long enough, and I shall submit no longer."

"We shall see about that," continued James. "Father will have a word to say about it, you will find."

"Yes, and he will probably say that you have abused me, and that you ought to control your temper and treat me better," responded Benjamin. "He always has decided in my favour, and I have no fears about his decision now."

It was not fair in Benjamin to take this advantage of his brother, and he knew it, but his resentment triumphed over his regard for right at the time. James returned his indenture only that he might be able to publish the paper unmolested. It was a deceitful arrangement in the first place, and Benjamin's use of the papers to assert his liberty was no more unfair and sinful than was James's device to make him the proprietor of the paper, and thus evade the law. James was paid in his own coin. He laid a plan to cheat the government, and he got cheated himself. He was snared in the work of his own hands. This, however, did not justify Benjamin in his course, as he afterwards saw, and frankly confessed.

Benjamin persisted in asserting his freedom, and James appealed to his father. After the latter had examined the affair, all the while knowing that James was passionate and overbearing, he decided against Benjamin. The advantage which the latter took of James to gain his freedom probably influenced Mr. Franklin to decide in favour of the former. This was unexpected by Benjamin, and was not received with a very good grace. It did not change his determination, however, and he was still resolved to be free. He refused to labour any more for his brother, and went forth to look for employment elsewhere. There were a number of other printers in the town, to whom he applied for work; but he found, to his surprise, that his brother had anticipated him, and been round to persuade them not to hire him.

"He has violated a solemn contract," said he to one, "and he will violate any contract he will make with you. Besides, if you refuse to hire him, he will be obliged to return and labour for me."

The printers all sympathized with James, and accordingly refused to give Benjamin work. He found himself in a very unpleasant situation on that account, without the means of earning his bread, and, in one sense, without a home, since he had disregarded his father's counsel in not returning to his brother. He learned, also, that some good people considered him no better than an infidel.

"Nothing less than the loosest sceptic," said one good man. "He hates the truth with all his heart, as much that he writes plainly shows. His influence in the community is very bad, and it is growing worse and worse."

Good people thus misjudged Benjamin. Some went so far as to call him an "atheist." His attacks upon the clergy and government, in his paper, created so much excitement, that he was understood to mean worse than he did.

All these things served to wean Benjamin from Boston, and he decided on seeking his fortune elsewhere. He embraced the first opportunity to confer with his old friend, John Collins, on the subject.

"John, I am going to New York," he said.

"To New York?" exclaimed John. "What has started you off there?"

"Enough to start anybody. I have been banged about long enough, and now can get no work at all; so I must go or starve."

"How so?" inquired John, "I don't understand you?"

"The case is just this," said Benjamin. "James has treated me very harshly for a long time, and I have submitted. But I had a good opportunity to make myself free, and I have improved it. When James was put into prison for libel, he returned me my indenture with a discharge written on the back, to show in case the government interfered with my publishing the paper. He did not mean, of course, that I should be released from my obligations to him; but he has treated me so unmercifully lately that I have taken advantage of the paper, and broken my engagement with him."

"You have got round him this time, certainly," said John. "How does he feel about it?"

"He has appealed to father, and father has decided against me, and advised me to go back; but I am not at all disposed to do it."

"I would work in some other printing-office," added John, "before I would go to New York."

"But I can get work nowhere else. I have been to every office, and they all refuse to employ me, because my brother went to them before me, and told his story, and made them promise not to hire me."

"I suppose he thought by so doing to compel you to come back to him," suggested John.

"I suppose so; but he will find himself mistaken. I shall go to New York as soon as I can get away."

"What does your father say about your going off so far?"

"I have said nothing to him about it, and do not intend to do so. He would stop my going at once if he knew it."

"How can you get away without letting him know it?"

"That remains to be seen," answered Benjamin. "I shall want some of your help about it, I guess."

"I am at your service," said John, "though it seems very little that I can do to hasten your flight;" but he had hardly uttered the last sentence before a new thought flashed upon his mind, and he added with great earnestness, "Yes, I can, too; I have seen the captain of that New York sloop in the harbour, and I can make a bargain with him to take you there."

"But he will want to know who I am, and will refuse to take me when he finds that I am a runaway."

"I can manage that, if you will leave it to me," answered John. "I will pledge you that he will never know that your name is Franklin."

"I agree, then, to commit myself to your care. See that you manage the affair well, for to New York I must go."

They parted; and John hurried away to see the aforesaid captain.

"Can you take a friend of mine to New York?" he asked.

"That depends on circumstances," answered the captain. "Who is your friend?"—a very natural inquiry,—precisely such a one as Benjamin thought would be made.

"He is a young man about my age, a printer, and he is going to New York to get work," replied John.

"Why don't he get work in Boston?" inquired the captain.

John saw that there was no evading the captain's questions, and so he suddenly resolved to fabricate a story, in other words, to tell a base lie.

"Well," said John, "if I must tell you the whole story, the case is this. He is a young fellow who has been flirting with a girl, who wants to marry him, and now her parents are determined that he shall marry her, and he is determined that he will not, and he proposes to remove secretly to New York. He would have come to see you himself, but it is not safe for him to appear out so publicly, and therefore he sent me to do the business."

A youth who can fabricate a falsehood so unblushingly as John did this is a candidate for ruin. The reader will not be surprised to learn, before the whole story is told, that he became a miserable, wicked man. This single lie proved that he was destitute of moral principle, and would do almost anything to carry his project.

For some unaccountable reason, the captain was taken with this device, and consented to carry Benjamin to New York. He arranged to receive him clandestinely, and to have him on his way before any suspicion of his plans was awakened.

John hastened to inform Benjamin of the success of his enterprise, and to congratulate him upon his fair prospect of getting away.

"Money is the next thing," said Benjamin. "I can't go without money. I must sell my books for something, though I dislike to part with them."

"They will sell quick enough," said John, "and will bring you a very pretty sum to start with."

Benjamin lost no time in disposing of his little library for what it would bring, and he managed to get his clothes together without exciting suspicion; and, with the assistance of John, he boarded the sloop privately just before she sailed.

"Good luck to you, Ben," said John, as they shook hands.

"Good bye," answered Benjamin with a heavy heart, just beginning to feel that he was going away from home. "See that you tell no tales out of school."

Thus they parted; and the sloop sailed for New York, where she arrived in three days. Benjamin did not know a person in that city, nor had he a single letter of recommendation to any one, and the money in his pocket was but a trifle. It was in October, 1723, that he arrived in New York. Think of a lad seventeen years of age running away from home, entering a large city without a solitary acquaintance, and possessing scarcely money enough to pay for a week's board! He must have carried some sad, lonely feelings in his heart along those strange streets, and possibly his conscience sorely upbraided him for his course.

Benjamin behaved very unwisely and wickedly in this affair. Although his brother was severely harsh in his treatment of him, it was not sufficient reason for his running away from home, and he was thoroughly convinced of this at an early day. Such an act is one of the most flagrant sins that a youth can commit, although circumstances may render it less guilty in some cases than in others. In the case of Benjamin, the unkind treatment which he received at the hand of his brother mitigated his sin, though it by no means excused it.

There is not a more unpleasant occurrence in the whole life of Benjamin Franklin than this quarrel with his brother. We charge the difficulty mainly upon James, of course; but this does not blot out the unpleasantness of the affair. A quarrel between brothers is always painful in the extreme, and is discreditable to all parties concerned. Dr. Watts has very beautifully written, for the admonition of little children, what older ones may well ponder:—

"Whatever brawls disturb the street,There should be peace at home:Where sisters dwell and brothers meet,Quarrels should never come.

"Birds in their little nests agree;And 'tis a shameful sight,When children of one familyFall out, and chide, and fight.

"Hard names, at first, and threat'ning words,That are but noisy breath,May grow to clubs and naked swords,To murder and to death."

At this crisis of Benjamin's life, it seemed as if he was on the highway to ruin. There is scarcely one similar case in ten, where the runaway escapes the vortex of degradation. Benjamin would not have been an exception, but for his early religious culture and the grace of God.

The case of William Hutton, who was the son of very poor parents, is not altogether unlike that of Benjamin Franklin. He was bound to his uncle for a series of years, but was treated by him so harshly that he ran away, at seventeen years of age. The record is, that "on the 12th day of July, 1741, the ill-treatment he received from his uncle, in the shape of a brutal flogging, with a birch-broom handle of white hazel, which almost killed him, caused him to run away." A dark prospect was before him, since "he had only twopence in his pocket, a spacious world before him, and no plan of operation." Yet he afterwards became an author of some celebrity, and a most exemplary and esteemed man. He lived to the age of ninety, his last days being gladdened by the reflection of having lived a useful life, and the consciousness of sharing the confidence of his fellow-men.

CHAPTER XVI.

ANOTHER TRIP AND ITS TRIALS.

ON arriving at New York, Benjamin applied to a well known printer, Mr. William Bradford, for work.

"Where are you from?" he inquired.

"From Boston," was Benjamin's reply.

"Used to the printing business?"

"Yes, that is my trade. I have worked at it several years."

"I am sorry I cannot employ you. Just now my business is small, and I have all the help I need."

"What do you think of the prospect of getting work at some other office in the town?" inquired Benjamin.

"Not very flattering, I am sorry to say. Dull times, my son, very dull indeed. But I can tell you where you can find employment, I think. My son carries on the printing business in Philadelphia, and one of his men died the other day. I think he would be glad to employ you."

"How far is it to Philadelphia?"

"It is a hundred miles," replied Mr. Bradford, "a much shorter distance than you have already travelled."

Franklin saving the Dutchman.—See page 149.

Benjamin looked somewhat disappointed when he found that Philadelphia was a hundred miles farther; still, he was after work, and he was determined to find it; so he made inquiries about the mode of conveyance, and left Mr. Bradford, thanking him for his kindness. Immediately he engaged a passage in a boat to Amboy, and made arrangements for his chest to be carried round by sea. He was less disheartened, probably, on account of the assurance of Mr. Bradford that his son would employ him. If he could procure work by travelling a hundred miles more, he would cheerfully do it, although a journey of a hundred miles then was about equal to one thousand now.

At the appointed time Benjamin went aboard, and the boat started. She had not proceeded far when a squall struck her, tore her rotten sails to pieces, and drove her upon Long Island. Before this, however, a drunken Dutchman, who was also a passenger, fell overboard, and would have lost his life but for the timely assistance of our printer-boy. Springing to the side of the boat, Benjamin reached over and seized him by the hair of his head as he rose, and drew him on board.

"He may thank you for saving his life," exclaimed one of the boatmen.

"He is too drunk for that," answered Benjamin. "It will sober him a little, however, I think. Halloo, here, you Dutchman!" (turning to the drunken man) "how do you like diving?"

The Dutchman mumbled over something, and pulling a book out of his pocket, asked Benjamin to dry it for him, which he promised to do. Soon the poor, miserable fellow was fast asleep, in spite of the wet and danger, and Benjamin examined the drenched volume, which proved to be Bunyan's Pilgrim's Progress, in Dutch, a favourite book of his a few years before. It was a very good companion for even a drunken Dutchman to have; but Benjamin could not but think that its contents were not so familiar to the unfortunate possessor as the bottle.

On approaching Long Island they found that there was no place to land, and the beach was very stony; so "they dropped anchor, and swung out their cable towards the shore." Some men came down to the shore and hallooed to them, and they returned the shout. Seeing some small boats lying along the shore, they cried out as loudly as possible, "A boat! a boat!" and made signs to them to come to their assistance; but the wind was so boisterous that neither party could understand the other.

After several fruitless attempts on both sides to be heard, and night coming on, the men on the shore went home, and left Benjamin and the boatmen to their perils.

"There is only one thing to be done," said the captain, "when we get into such a predicament."

"What is that?" asked Benjamin.

"To do nothing but wait patiently till the wind abates," answered the captain, rather coolly.

"Then let us turn in with the Dutchman to sleep," said one of the boatmen. "It isn't best for him to have all the good things."

All agreed to this, and soon they were crowded into the hatches, Benjamin among the number. But the spray broke over the head of the boat so much that the water leaked through upon them, until they were about as wet as the Dutchman. This was hard fare for Benjamin, who had been accustomed to a comfortable bed and regular sleep. It was impossible for him to rest in such a plight, and he had all the more time *to think*. He thought of home, and the friends he had left behind, of the comfortable quarters he had exchanged for his present wet and perilous berth, and he began to feel that he had *paid too dear for his whistle*. Runaways usually feel thus sooner or later, since few of them ever realize their anticipations.

The cold, dreary night wore away slowly, and the wind continued to howl, and the breakers to dash and roar, until after the dawn of the following morning. Benjamin was never more rejoiced to see daylight appear than he was after that dismal and perilous night. It was the more pleasant to him because the wind began to abate, and there was a fairer prospect of reaching their place of destination. As soon as the tumult of the wind and waves had subsided, they weighed anchor, and steered for Amboy, where they arrived just before night, "having been thirty hours on the water without victuals, or any drink but a bottle of filthy rum."

In the evening Benjamin found himself feverish, having taken a severe cold by the exposure of the previous night. With a hot head and a heavy heart he retired to rest, first, however, drinking largely of cold water, because he had somewhere read that cold water was good for fever. This was one of the advantages he derived from his early habit of reading. But for his taste for reading, which led him to spend his leisure moments in poring over books, he might never have known this important fact, which perhaps saved him a fit of sickness. Availing himself of this knowledge, he drank freely of water before he retired, and the consequence was, that he sweat most of the night, and arose the next morning comparatively well. So much advantage from loving books!

Boys never have occasion to deplore the habit of reading, provided their books are well chosen. They usually find that they are thrice paid for all the time spent in this way. Sooner or later they begin to reap the benefits of so wise a course. A few years since, a young man was travelling in the State of Maine, procuring subscribers to a newspaper. On passing a certain farm, he observed some bricks of a peculiar colour, and he traced them to their clay-bed, and satisfied himself that the material could be applied to a more valuable purpose than that of making bricks. He at once purchased the farm for three hundred pounds, and, on his return to Boston, sold one half of it for eight hundred pounds. The secret of his success lay in a bit of knowledge he acquired at school. He had given some attention to geology and chemistry, and the little knowledge he had gleaned therefrom enabled him to discover the nature of the clay on the farm. Thus, even a little knowledge gleaned from a book in a single leisure half-hour, will sometimes prove the key to a valuable treasure; much more valuable than the farm which the young man purchased. For this pecuniary benefit is, after all, the least important advantage derived from reading. The discipline of the mind and heart, and the refined and elevated pleasure which it secures, are far more desirable than any pecuniary good it bestows. A little reading, also, sometimes gives an impulse to the mind in the direction of learning and renown. It was the reading of Echard's Roman History, which Gibbon met with while on a visit to Wiltshire, that opened before him the historic path to distinction.

Let the reader consider these things. Never say, as hundred's of boys do, "I hate books, and wish that I was not obliged to go to school. There is no use in reading and studying so much; we shall get along just as well without it." This class of boys usually will have to regret, under mortifying circumstances, in later life, that they wasted their early opportunities to acquire knowledge. Sir Walter Scott, in his boyhood, joined in the tirade of idlers against books; but in manhood he said: "If it should ever fall to the lot of youth to peruse these pages, let such readers remember that it is with the deepest regret that I recollect, in my manhood, the opportunities of learning which I neglected in my youth; that through every part of my literary career I have felt pinched and hampered by my own ignorance; and I would at this moment give half the reputation I have had the good fortune to acquire, if by so doing I could rest the remaining part upon a sound foundation of learning and science."

But we have lost sight of Benjamin. We left him at the tavern in Amboy, after having passed the night in a cold-water sweat, ready for another start on his journey. Burlington was fifty miles from Amboy, and there was no public conveyance, so that he was obliged to go on foot, expecting to find a boat there bound for Philadelphia. It was raining hard, and yet he started upon the journey, and trudged on through the storm and the mud, eager to see Burlington. He was thoroughly drenched before he had travelled five miles, and, in this condition, he walked on rapidly till noon, when he came to a "poor inn," and stopped. Being wet and tired, he resolved to remain there until the next day. The innkeeper's suspicions were awakened by Benjamin's appearance, and he questioned him rather closely.

"Where are you from, my lad?"

"From Boston, sir."

"Hey! and away off here so far? quite a youngster for such a trip. What's your name?"

"My name is Benjamin Franklin, and I am going to Philadelphia after work."

"No work in Boston I 'spose, hey? How long since you left home?"

"About a week. I did not expect to go farther than New York when I started, but I could get no work there."

"No work, hey? what sort of work are you after that you find it so scarce?"

"I am a printer by trade, and I hope to get into a printing-office in Philadelphia."

"Wall, you are a pretty young one to go so far; I would hardly be willing that a son of mine should make such a trip alone, printer or no printer."

Benjamin saw that he was suspected of being a runaway, and he felt very uncomfortable. He managed, however, to answer all questions without satisfying the curiosity of the family. He ate and slept there, and on the following morning proceeded on his journey, and by night was within eight or ten miles of Burlington. Here he stopped at an inn kept by one Dr. Brown, "an ambulating quack doctor." He was a very social and observing man, and soon discovered that Benjamin was a youth of unusual intelligence for one of his age. He conversed with him freely about Boston and other places, and gave a particular account of some foreign countries which he had visited. In this way he made Benjamin's brief stay with him very pleasant, and they became friends for life, meeting many times thereafter on friendly terms.

The next morning he reluctantly bade the doctor good bye, and proceeded to Burlington, where he expected to find a boat. In the suburbs of the town he bought some gingerbread of an old woman who kept a shop, and walked on, eating it as he went. To his great disappointment, on reaching the wharf, he found the boat had gone, and there would not be another until Tuesday. It was now Saturday, and his money would not hold out if he should get boarded at a public-house till then. What should he do? After some reflection, he determined to go back to the old lady of whom he bought his gingerbread, as he liked her appearance very well, and ask her advice. So back he went.

"Ah! back again?" said she, as he entered her shop. "Want more gingerbread I 'spose?"

"No," answered Benjamin. "I was going to take the boat to Philadelphia, but it has gone, and there is not another to go until Tuesday."

"Dear me!" exclaimed the kind-hearted woman; "if that ain't too bad. What kin ye du?"

"That is what I want to ask you. Is there any other conveyance to Philadelphia?"

"No, and all ye has to du is to make the best on't."

"And what is that? That is just what I want to know,—the best thing for me to do in such a case."

"What ye goin' to Philadelphy for?" inquired the old lady.

"I am going after work. I am a printer, and want to find work in a printing-office."

"A printer," exclaimed the woman, who had probably never seen one before. "Dear me, yer fortin is made to set up business in this ere town. There is nothing of the like here."

"I have nothing to set up the business with here," replied Benjamin. "I would as lief work here as in Philadelphia, if the way was open."

The woman did not know what was necessary in setting up a printing establishment. That types and a press were indispensable articles in such business she did not dream. She thought, doubtless, that he carried all necessary fixtures with him in his pockets.

"Well, then, I'll lodge ye till Tuesday for ——" (naming the sum).

"I will stay with you, then, and make the best of it," he replied.

He found himself in very good quarters, and his host proved herself to be very kind and hospitable. He took dinner with her, and remained about the shop until towards night, when he walked forth to view the place. In his walk he came round to the river, and as he approached it, he discovered a boat with several people in it, and he hailed them.

"Whither bound?"

"To Philadelphia."

"Can you take me in? I was too late for the boat to-day."

"As well as not," a voice replied; and the boat was turned to receive its additional passenger. There was no wind, so that they were obliged to depend on rowing for progress. Benjamin now found a rare opportunity to exercise the skill at rowing which he cultivated in Boston. He was so elated with the prospect of proceeding on his way to Philadelphia, that he thought neither of the fatigue of rowing, nor of the wonder of the old lady in the shop at the unexpected disappearance of her boarder. He did not mean to treat her disrespectfully, for he considered her a very clever woman, but the boat could not wait for him to return and pay her his compliments.

Whether she ever learned what became of him, or that he grew up to be Dr. Franklin, the great philosopher, we have no means of knowing. Doubtless she concluded that she had not entertained an "angel unawares," but had rather aided an undeserving fellow in pursuing a vicious course,—which was not true.

The boat went on. Benjamin rowed with strong resolution, taking his turn with others, until midnight, when one of the company said: "We must have passed the city. It can't be that we have been so long getting to it."

"That is impossible," said another. "We must have seen it, if we had passed it."

"Well, I shall row no more," added the first speaker. "I know that Philadelphia is not so far off as this."

"Let us put for the shore," said a third person, "and find out where we are, if possible."

"Agreed," replied several voices; and so saying they rowed toward the shore, and entered a small creek, where they landed near an old fence, the rails of which furnished them with fuel for a fire. They were very chilly, it being a frosty night of October, and they found the fire very grateful. They remained there till daylight, when one of the company knew that the place was "Cooper's Creek," a few miles above the "City of Brotherly Love." Immediately they made preparations to continue their journey, which had not been altogether unpleasant, and they were soon in full view of the city, where they arrived between eight and nine o'clock on Sunday morning. They landed at Market Street Wharf. Taking out his money, which consisted of one unbroken dollar, and a shilling in copper coin, he offered the latter to the boatmen for his passage.

"Not a cent, my good fellow," said one of them, "you worked your passage, and did it well, too."

"But you *must* take it," responded Benjamin. "You are quite welcome to all the rowing I have done. I am glad enough to get here by rowing and paying my passage too. But for your coming along to take me in, I should have been obliged to stay in Burlington until next Tuesday;" and he fairly forced the shilling into their hands. This manifested a spirit of generosity, for which Benjamin was always distinguished. He was no mean, niggardly fellow, not he. Although he was in a stranger city, and had but a single dollar left on which to live until he could earn something by daily toil, yet he cheerfully gave the change for his passage. He felt grateful to them for taking him in, and he gave expression to his gratitude in this generous way. It was noble, too, in the boatman to refuse to take the shilling. It was only on his insisting upon their receiving it, that they consented to take it. A kind-hearted, generous set of fellows were in that boat, and Benjamin was not inferior to one of them in that respect. Bidding them good morning, he walked up Market Street, where he met a boy eating some bread.

"Where did you get your bread, boy?" he inquired.

"Over to the baker's, there," he replied, pointing to a shop that was near by.

Benjamin was very tired and hungry, having eaten nothing since he dined with the old shopwoman in Burlington, on the day before; and, for this reason, the boy's bread was very tempting. Besides, he had made many a meal of dry bread when he boarded himself in Boston; and now it was not hard at all for him to breakfast on unbuttered bread, minus both tea and coffee. He hastened to the bakery, and found it open.

"Have you biscuit?" he inquired, meaning such as he was accustomed to eat in Boston.

"We make nothing of the kind," answered the proprietor.

"You may give me a three-penny loaf, then."

"We have none."

Benjamin began to think that he should have to go hungry still, since he did not know the names or prices of the kinds of bread made in Philadelphia. But in a moment he recovered himself, and said: "Then give me three-pennyworth of any sort."

Miss Read's first Glimpse of her future Husband.—See page 162.

To his surprise the baker gave him three great puffy rolls, enough to satisfy half a dozen hungry persons. He looked at it, scarcely knowing at first what he could do with so much, but, as "necessity is the mother of invention," he soon discovered a way of disposing of it. He put a roll under each arm, and taking a third in his hand he proceeded to eat it, as he continued his way up Market Street.

Let the reader stop here, and take a view of Benjamin Franklin, the runaway youth, as he made his first appearance in the city of Philadelphia. See him trudging up Market Street with his worn, dirty clothes (his best suit having been sent round by sea), his pockets stuffed out with shirts and stockings, and a "puffy roll" under each arm, and a third in his hand of which he is eating! A comical appearance certainly! It is not very probable that this runaway Benjamin will ever become "Minister Plenipotentiary to the Court of France," or surprise the world by his philosophical discoveries! There is much more probability that he will live in some obscure printing-office, and die, "unknown, unhonoured, and unsung." Who wonders that a young lady, Miss Read, who was standing in the door of her father's residence as Benjamin passed, thought he made a very awkward and ridiculous appearance? She little thought she was taking a bird's-eye view of her future husband, as the youth with the rolls of bread under his arm proved to be. But just then he cared more for bread than he did for her; some years after, the case was reversed, and he cared more for her than he did for bread.

Turning down Chestnut Street he continued to walk until he came round to the wharf where he landed. Being thirsty, he went to the boat for water, where he found the woman and child who came down the river with them on the previous night, waiting to go further.

"Are you hungry?" he inquired of the child, who looked wistfully at his bread.

"We are both very hungry," answered the woman, speaking for herself and child.

"I have satisfied my hunger," said Benjamin, "and you may have the rest of my bread if you would like it," at the same time passing both rolls to her.

"You are very kind indeed," responded the woman. "I thank you much for it;"—all of which was as good pay for the bread as Benjamin wanted. This was another instance of the generosity for which he was distinguished throughout his whole life. An American statesman said of him, in a eulogy delivered in Boston: "No form of personal suffering or social evil escaped his attention, or appealed in vain for such relief or remedy as his prudence could suggest, or his purse supply. From that day of his early youth, when, a wanderer from his home and friends in a strange place, he was seen sharing his rolls with a poor woman and child, to the last act of his public life, when he signed that well known memorial to Congress, a spirit of earnest and practical benevolence runs like a golden thread along his whole career."

He then walked up the street again, and found well-dressed people going to church. Joining in the current, notwithstanding his appearance, he went with them into the large Quaker meeting-house that stood near the market. He took his seat, and waited for the services to begin, either not knowing what Quakers did at meeting, or else being ignorant that he was among this sect. As nothing was said, and he was weary and exhausted with the labours and watchings of the previous night, he became drowsy, and soon dropped into a sweet sleep. His nap might have proved a very unfortunate event for him, but for the kindness of a wide-awake Quaker. For he did not wake up when the meeting closed, and the congregation might have dispersed, and the sexton locked him in, without disturbing his slumbers. But the kind-hearted Quaker moved his spirit by giving him a gentle rap on the shoulder. He started up, somewhat surprised that the service was over, and passed out with the crowd. Soon after, meeting a fine-looking young Quaker, who carried his heart in his face, Benjamin inquired, "Can you tell me where a stranger can get a night's lodging?"

"Here," answered the Quaker, "is a house where they receive strangers" (pointing to the sign of the Three Mariners near which they stood), "but it is not a reputable one; if thee will walk with me I will show thee a better one."

"I will be obliged to you for doing so," answered Benjamin. "I was never in Philadelphia before, and am not acquainted with one person here."

The Quaker conducted him to Water Street, and showed him the Crooked Billet,—a house where he might be accommodated. Benjamin thanked him for his kindness, entered the house, and called for dinner and a room. While sitting at the dinner-table, his host asked, "Where are you from?"

"I am from Boston?"

"Boston!" exclaimed the host, with some surprise. "How long since you left home?"

This question being answered, he continued, "Have you friends in Philadelphia?"

"None at all. I do not know a single person here."

"What did you come here for?"

"I came to get work in a printing-office. I am a printer by trade."

"How old are you?"

"I am seventeen years old, sir," replied Benjamin, just beginning to perceive that the man suspected him of being a runaway.

"And came all the way from Boston alone?"

"Yes, sir!"

Benjamin closed the conversation as soon as he could conveniently, after perceiving that his appearance had excited suspicions, and went to his room, where he lay down and slept till six o'clock in the evening, when he was called to supper. He went to bed again very early, and was soon locked in the embrace of "nature's sweet restorer, balmy sleep."

CHAPTER XVII.

GETTING WORK.

AFTER a good night's sleep, Benjamin arose and dressed himself as neatly as he could with his old clothes, and repaired to Andrew Bradford's printing-office.

"Ah! then you have arrived," said an old gentleman, rising to salute him as he entered. "I reached here first."

"Oh, it is Mr. Bradford!" exclaimed Benjamin, surprised at meeting the old printer whom he saw in New York, and who directed him to his son, Andrew Bradford, of Philadelphia. "I did not expect to meet you here."

"I suppose not. I started off unexpectedly, and came all the way on horseback. But I am glad that you have reached here safely. This is a young man from Boston" (addressing his son and introducing Benjamin), "after work in a printing-office, and I directed him to you. Franklin is your name, I believe."

"Yes, sir! Benjamin Franklin."

Mr. Bradford received him very cordially, and being about to eat breakfast, he said: "Come, it is my breakfast hour, and you shall be welcome to the table. We can talk this matter over at the table;"—and Benjamin accepted the invitation.

"I told this young man," said the old printer from New York, "that one of your men died a short time since, and you would want a printer to take his place."

"That is true," replied Mr. Andrew Bradford. "I did want another hand to take his place, but I hired one only a few days since. I am sorry to disappoint this youth who has come so far for work."

"Is there another printing-office here?" asked Benjamin.

"Yes; a man by the name of Keimer has just commenced the business, and I think he would be glad to employ you."

"I must get work somewhere," added Benjamin, "for I have spent nearly all my money in getting here."

"If he will not employ you," added Mr. Bradford, kindly, "you may lodge at my house, and I will give you a little work from time to time until business is better."

"That will be a great favour to me," answered Benjamin, "for which I shall be very thankful;" and he really felt more grateful to Mr. Bradford for the offer than his words indicated.

"I will go with you to see Mr. Keimer," said old Mr. Bradford from New York. "Perhaps I can be of some service to you in securing a place."

Benjamin began to think he had fallen into very obliging hands; so he followed their advice, and went with his aged friend to see the newly-established printer. On arriving at the office, they met Mr. Keimer, and old Mr. Bradford introduced their business by saying: "Neighbour, I have brought to see you a young man of your business; perhaps you may want such a one."

"That depends on his qualifications," answered Mr. Keimer. "How long have you worked at the business?" he inquired, turning to Benjamin.

"Several years, sir."

"Do you understand all parts of it so that you can go on with it?"

"I think I do; you can try me and satisfy yourself."

"Take this composing-stick and let me see whether you are competent or not," said Keimer.

Benjamin proceeded to exhibit his skill at the work, and very soon satisfied Keimer that he had told the truth.

"Very well done," said Keimer. "I will employ you as soon as I have sufficient work to warrant such a step. At present I have nothing for you to do."

Here Benjamin saw the advantage of having attended to his business closely, so as to learn thoroughly the work he was to do. Some boys perform their work in just a passable way, not caring particularly whether it is well done, if they can only "pass muster." But not so with Benjamin. He sought to understand the business to which he attended, and to do as well as possible the work he undertook. The consequence was that he was a thorough workman, and in five minutes he was able to satisfy Keimer of the fact. This was greatly in his favour; and such a young man is never long out of business.

Turning to Bradford, Keimer said, supposing him to be a Philadelphian who wished him well in his new enterprise: "What do you think of my prospects here, sir? Do you think I shall succeed in my business?"

"That will depend upon your own exertions and business talents," was Bradford's reply.

"I shall do all in my power to draw the business of the town," added Keimer; "and I think I can do it."

"But how can you expect to get all the business when there is another printer here, who has been established some time?"

Keimer answered this last inquiry by disclosing his plans, as Bradford quietly drew him out on every point, until he learned how he was calculating to command all the business, and run his son out. Nor did Keimer dream that he was conversing with the father of the other printer whom he designed to deprive of his livelihood. All the while Benjamin stood and listened to their conversation, perceiving that Mr. Bradford was shrewdly learning Keimer's plans for his son's benefit.

"Did you not know that man?" inquired Benjamin, after Bradford left, leaving him in the office.

"No; but I thought that he was one of the town's people who wished me well in my business, and therefore came in to introduce you."

"It is not so," replied Benjamin. "That was the father of Andrew Bradford, your neighbour, the printer. He carries on printing in New York."

"It can't be!" exclaimed Keimer, astonished at this bit of news, and startled at the thought of having made known his plans to a competitor.

"It *can* be," replied Benjamin. "He is certainly Bradford, the New York printer, and father of Andrew Bradford, the printer of this town."

"How happened it that he should come here with you?"

"I can tell you in few words," said Benjamin; and he went on and told him of his going to New York, and how he happened to come to Philadelphia, and meet Mr. Bradford there, and finally how he found his way to Keimer's office.

"It will learn me a good lesson," said Keimer. "When I divulge secrets to another man whom I don't know, I shall not be in my right mind."

Benjamin spent a short time in looking over Keimer's office, and found that his press was old and damaged, and his fount of English types nearly worn out. Possessing much more ingenuity than Keimer, and understanding a printing-press much better, he went to work, and in a short time put it into decent order for service. Keimer was composing an Elegy on Aquila Rose, an excellent young man who worked for Bradford, and who had recently died; and he agreed to send for Benjamin to print it off when it was ready. With this arrangement, Benjamin returned to Mr. Bradford to eat and lodge. A few days after he received a message from

Keimer that the Elegy was ready to be printed. From that time Keimer provided him with work.

"You must have another boarding-place," said Keimer to him one day. Benjamin was still boarding at Bradford's, and this was not agreeable to Keimer.

"Just as you please," answered Benjamin; "I am satisfied to board there or go elsewhere."

"I can get you boarded with an acquaintance of mine, I think, where you will find it very pleasant. I am confident that you will like it better there than at Mr. Bradford's."

"I will go there, if you think it is best," added Benjamin. "My chest has arrived, and I can look a little more respectable now than I could before."

The result was, that he went to board at Mr. Read's, the father of the young lady who stood in the door when he passed on the aforesaid Sunday morning with a roll of bread under each arm. His appearance was much improved by this time, so that even Miss Read saw that he was an intelligent promising young man.

We learn one or two things about Benjamin from the foregoing, which the reader may ponder with benefit to himself. In the first place, he must have been very observing. He understood the construction of a printing-press so well, that he could put an old one into running order, youth as he was, when its proprietor was unable to do it. This is more remarkable, because he was not obliged to study the mechanism of a printing-press in order to work it. Doubtless many a person operates this and other machines without giving any particular attention to their structure. But a class of minds are never satisfied until they understand whatever commands their attention. They are inquisitive to learn the philosophy of things. It was so with Benjamin, and this characteristic proved a valuable element of his success. It was the secret of his inventions and discoveries thereafter. It was so with Stephenson, of whom we have spoken before. As soon as he was appointed plugman of an engine, at seventeen years of age, he began to study its construction. In his leisure hours, he took it to pieces and put it together again several times, in order to understand it. So of William Hutton, whose name is mentioned in another place. Encouraged by a couplet which he read in Dyce's Spelling-book—

"Despair of nothing that you would attain,Unwearied diligence your end will gain," he sought to master everything that he undertook. One day he borrowed a dulcimer, and made one by it. With no other tools than the hammer-key, and pliers of the stocking-frame for hammer and pincers, his pocket-knife, and a one-pronged fork that served as spring, awl, and gimlet, he made a capital dulcimer, which he sold for sixteen shillings. Here were both observation and perseverance, though not more finely developed than they were in the character of young Benjamin Franklin.

Another important truth is learned from the foregoing, namely, that Benjamin was not proud. A sight of him passing up Market Street, with three large rolls of bread, is proof of this; or his appearance in the street and Quaker church in his everyday garb, because his best suit was "coming round by sea," is equally significant. How many boys of his age would have stayed away from church until the "best clothes" arrived! How many would seek for some concealment of their poverty, if possible, in similar circumstances! But these were small matters to Benjamin, in comparison with finding employment and earning a livelihood. He had a destiny to work out, and in working that he must do as he could, and not always as he would. He cared not for the laughs and jeers of those who could dress better and live more sumptuously than himself, since it was absolutely necessary for him to dress as he did, in order to "make his ends meet." He might have followed the example of some young men, and run into debt, in order to "cut a dash;" but he believed then, as he wrote afterwards, that "lying rides on debt's back," and that it is "better to go to bed supperless than to rise in debt;" or, as he expressed himself in other maxims, "Those have a short Lent who owe money to be paid at Easter," and "It is easier to build two chimneys than to keep one in fuel."

CHAPTER XVIII.

NEWS FROM HOME, AND RETURN.

HITHERTO Benjamin had lived contentedly in Philadelphia, striving to forget Boston and old familiar scenes as much as possible. No one at home knew of his whereabouts, except his old friend Collins, who kept the secret well. One day, however, a letter came to his address, and the superscription looked so familiar that Benjamin's hand fairly trembled as he broke the seal. It proved to be from his brother-in-law, Robert Homes, "master of a sloop that traded between Boston and Delaware." He came to Newcastle, it seems, about forty miles from Philadelphia, and, hearing of Benjamin's place of residence, he sat down and wrote him a letter, telling him of the deep sorrow into which his departure had plunged his parents, who still were wholly ignorant of his fate, and exhorting him to return home to his friends, who would welcome him kindly. The letter was a strong appeal to his feelings.

Benjamin sat down and replied to the letter, stating his reasons in full for leaving Boston, giving an account of his present circumstances and prospects, and closing by expressing kind feelings for all the loved ones at home, but declining to return.

Not many days after Benjamin wrote and sent his letter, an unusual scene transpired at the office. He was at work near the window, when, on looking out, he saw Governor Keith approaching.

"The Governor is coming in," said he to Keimer.

Keimer looked out of the window, and saw that it was so, whereupon he hurried down to the door, not a little excited by the thought of waiting upon the Governor, supposing, of course, that he was coming in to see him.

"Does Benjamin Franklin work for you?" inquired the Governor.

"He does," answered Keimer, both astonished and perplexed by the inquiry. What he could want of him he could not imagine.

"Can I see him?" asked the Governor.

"Certainly; walk in." The Governor and Colonel French, who was with him, were ushered into the presence of Benjamin.

"I am happy to make the acquaintance of a young man of your abilities," he said to him. "I regret that you did not report yourself to me long ago."

Benjamin was too much astonished at the unexpected interview to be able to reply; and the Governor went on to say, that "he called to invite him to an interview at the tavern." Benjamin was more perplexed than ever, and Keimer stared with amazement. But after some hesitation, arising from sudden surprise, Benjamin consented to go with the Governor, and was soon seated with him and Colonel French in a room of the tavern at the corner of Third Street.

"I called to see you," said the Governor, "respecting the printing business in this town. I understand that you are well acquainted with it in all its branches, and, from my knowledge of your abilities, I think you would succeed admirably in setting up the business for yourself. Our printers here are ignorant and inefficient, and we must have more competent men to do the government work."

How the Governor knew so much about his qualifications for the business, Benjamin could not divine. He replied, however, "I have nothing to commence business with, and it will require some capital. My father might assist me if he were disposed; but I have no reason to think that he would."

"I will write to him upon the subject," said the Governor, "and perhaps he may be persuaded. I can show him the advantages of such an enterprise to yourself and the public, so that he cannot doubt the practicability of the thing."

"There are two printers here already," continued Benjamin; "and a third one would hardly be supported."

"A third one, who understands the business as you do," responded the Governor, "would command the chief business of the town in a short time. I will pledge you all the public printing of the government."

"And I will pledge the same for the government of Delaware," said Colonel French of Newcastle.

"There can be no doubt on this point," continued Governor Keith. "You had better decide to return to Boston by the first vessel, and take a letter from me to your father."

"I will so decide at once, if such is your judgment in the matter," replied Benjamin.

"Then it is understood," added his Excellency, "that you will repair to Boston in the first vessel that sails. In the mean time, you must continue to work for Mr. Keimer, keeping the object of this interview a profound secret."

Having made this arrangement, they separated, and Benjamin returned to the printing-office, scarcely knowing how he should evade the anticipated inquisitiveness of Keimer respecting the interview; but he succeeded in keeping the secret. His mind, however, laboured much upon the question, how Governor Keith should know anything about him, a poor obscure printer-boy. It was not until he returned to Boston that this mystery was solved. Then he learned that Keith was present at Newcastle when his brother-in-law received his (Benjamin's) letter, and Captain Homes read it aloud to him.

"How old is he?" asked the Governor.

"Seventeen," replied Captain Homes.

"Only seventeen! I am surprised that a youth of that age should write so well. He must be an uncommon boy."

Captain Homes assured him that he was a very competent youth, and possessed abilities that qualified him for almost any place. Here was the secret of Keith's interest in the printer-boy, but of which the latter knew nothing until he met his brother-in-law in Boston.

Before an opportunity offered for Benjamin to go to Boston, Governor Keith frequently sent for him to dine with him, on which occasions he conversed with him in a very friendly and familiar way. It was quite unusual for a boy of seventeen years to become the frequent guest of a Governor, and no wonder he was almost bewildered by the unexpected attention. Some would have become vain and proud in consequence of such attentions; but Benjamin bore the honours meekly.

About the last of April, 1724, a small vessel offered for Boston. Benjamin made arrangements to go, took leave of Keimer as if going to visit his friends, and, with Keith's letter to his father, sailed. The vessel had a boisterous time at sea, but after a fortnight's voyage she entered Boston harbour. Benjamin had been absent seven months, and his parents had not heard a word from him. His brother-in-law had not returned from Newcastle, nor written to them about his knowledge of Benjamin. The reader may well imagine, then, that he took them all by surprise. His poor mother had laid his absence to heart so much, that it had worn upon her, and his return was to her almost like life from the dead. She was overjoyed, and no language could express her delight as she looked into the face of her long-lost Benjamin. His father was not less rejoiced, although he had a different way of showing it. Indeed, all the family, except his brother James, gave him a most cordial and affectionate welcome. He did not return ragged and penniless, as runaways generally do, but he was clad in a new and handsome suit, carried a watch in his pocket, and had about five pounds sterling in silver in his purse. He never looked half so genteel and neat in his life, and certainly never commanded so much money at one time before.

Before his brother James heard of his arrival, Benjamin hastened to the printing-office, and startled him by suddenly standing before him. James stopped his work, saluted him in rather a reserved manner, and, after surveying him from head to foot, turned to his work again. It was rather a cold reception on the whole, but not altogether unexpected to Benjamin. A brother who had driven him away by his harsh treatment could hardly be expected to welcome him back with a very warm heart.

The journeymen were delighted to see him, and they were very inquisitive.

"Where have you been, Ben?" asked one.

"To Philadelphia," he answered.

"What kind of a place is it?"

"It is one of the finest places I ever saw. I like it better than Boston."

"Going back?" inquired a second person.

"Yes; and very soon, too," he replied. "That is the place for the printing business."

"What kind of money do you have there?" inquired Another. There was no established currency in the country at that time, and his interrogator wanted to know what they used in Philadelphia.

Instead of replying directly, Benjamin drew the silver from his pocket, and spread it out before them. It was quite a curiosity to them, as they used only paper money in Boston; and, besides, it caused them to think that their old associate had fallen upon lucky days.

"You made a lucky hit, Ben, this time," said one.

"Heavy stuff to carry about," suggested a second. "A man would want a wheelbarrow if he had much of it."

"Perhaps you would accept of the wheelbarrow and silver together, rather than have neither," responded Benjamin.

By this time Benjamin's watch was discovered, and there was a general desire to see it; so he laid it down before them, while his brother appeared "grum and sullen."

"That is a convenient companion," said Benjamin, as he laid it down.

"And you can afford to have such things," added one of the number, "because you save your money, and don't spend it for pleasure, drink, and luxuries."

"Ben has fared so well," said one, "that it belongs to him to treat the company." As we have said before, the use of intoxicating drinks was general at that time, and when old friends met, it was common to signalize the occasion by the use of such beverage. Had Benjamin lived at this day, with his temperate habits, he would have refused to pander to their appetite for strong drink, and suggested some other kind of treat. But, living as he did when there were no temperance societies, and no alarm at the growing evils of intoxication, he accepted the proposal in his accustomed generous way.

"There is a dollar," said he, throwing out a dollar in silver, "take that, and drink what you please for old acquaintance sake." Then, pocketing his watch and money, he took his leave.

His brother was greatly incensed at this visit, and regarded it in the light of an insult. His mother endeavoured to bring him to terms of reconciliation with Benjamin, but in vain.

"You are brothers," said she, "and you ought to behave towards each other as brothers. It is very painful to me to think of your hostility to Benjamin, and I do hope that you will forget the past, and be true to each other in future."

"Never," replied James. "He insulted me so directly before my workmen the other day, that I shall not forget nor forgive it."

James was mistaken in his view of Benjamin's intention. The latter did not mean to insult him at the office. He would have been glad of a cordial welcome from James, and his feelings were such that he would have rejoicingly blotted out the recollection of his former ill-treatment, had James met him as a brother.

Benjamin took the first opportunity to make known to his father the object and circumstances of his visit home, and to hand him the Governor's letter, which he received with manifest surprise, though he evidently doubted whether it was genuine. For several days he entered into no conversation about the matter, as he did not exactly know what to make of it. Just then Captain Homes returned, and Mr. Franklin showed him the letter of Governor Keith, and inquired if he knew the man.

"I have met him," replied Captain Homes, "and was pleased with his appearance. I think it would be well for Benjamin to follow his advice."

"He cannot be a man of much discretion," continued Mr. Franklin, "to think of setting up a boy in business who lacks three years of arriving at his majority. The project does not strike me favourably at all."

"He was much taken with Benjamin's abilities," added Captain Homes, "by a letter which I received from him at Newcastle, and which I read to him, as he was present when I received it."

"His letters may be well enough, for aught I know; but a youth of his age, though his abilities be good, has not sufficient judgment to conduct business for himself. I shall not give my consent to such a wild scheme."

Mr. Franklin replied to Governor Keith's letter, and thanked him kindly for the patronage he offered his son, but declining to set up a youth in a business of so much importance.

"I am rejoiced," said he to Benjamin, just before the latter started to go back, "that you have conducted yourself so well as to secure the esteem of Sir William Keith. Your appearance, too, shows that you have been industrious and economical, all of which pleases me very much. I should advise you to go back, and think no more of going into business for yourself until you are of age. By industry, economy, and perseverance you will be able to command the means of establishing business then. As yet you are too young. I should be glad to have you remain here with your brother, if he could be reconciled to you; but as it is, you shall have my approbation and blessing in returning to Philadelphia."

Anecdote of Dr. Mather and Franklin—Humility "beaten in!"—See page 186.

It was during this visit to Boston that he called upon the celebrated Dr. Increase Mather, to whose preaching he had been accustomed to listen. The Doctor received him kindly, and introduced him into his library, where they chatted in a familiar way for some time. When Benjamin rose to go out, "Come this way," said the Doctor, "I will show you a nearer passage out,"—pointing him to a narrow passage, with a beam crossing it over head. They were still talking, the Doctor following behind, and Benjamin partly turned around toward him.

"*Stoop! stoop!*" shouted the Doctor.

Benjamin did not understand what he meant, until his head struck against the beam with considerable force.

"There," said the Doctor, laughing, "you are young, and have the world before you; stoop as you go through it, and you may miss many hard thumps."

Nearly seventy years after, the recipient of this counsel wrote:—

"This advice, thus beaten into my head, has frequently been of use to me; and I often think of it, when I see pride mortified, and misfortunes brought upon people by their carrying their heads too high."

Benjamin's old companion, Collins, was delighted with his account of Philadelphia, and resolved to accompany him thither on his return. He was a clerk in the post-office; but he gave up his situation for the more alluring prospects of a residence in Pennsylvania. He started two or three days before Benjamin, as he wanted to stop and make a visit in Rhode Island, having previously gathered up his books, "which were a pretty collection in mathematics and philosophy," and packed them to go, with Benjamin's baggage, around by sea to New York, where they would meet.

CHAPTER XIX.

BACK AGAIN.

ON his return, Benjamin sailed in a sloop to New York, where he had arranged to meet Collins. They put in at Newport on business, where he had a good opportunity to visit his brother John, who had been married and settled there some years. He received a very hearty and affectionate welcome from his brother, who was always kind and true to him. His stay was short, as he must go when the sloop did, but he made the most of it, and enjoyed himself much during the short time. Just before he left Newport, a friend of his brother, a Mr. Vernon, requested him to collect a debt for him in Pennsylvania, of about thirty-five pounds currency, and use the money as he pleased until he should call for it. Accordingly, he gave Benjamin an order to receive it.

At Newport they took in a number of passengers, among whom was a Quaker lady and her servants, and two young women. Benjamin was very attentive in assisting the Quaker lady about her baggage, for which she was very thankful. He soon became acquainted with the two young women, and they laughed and chatted together. They were handsomely attired, appeared intelligent, and were extremely sociable. The motherly Quaker lady saw that there was a growing familiarity between them, and she called Benjamin aside, feeling for him somewhat as she would for a son, and said: "Young man, I am concerned for thee, as thou hast no friend with thee, and seems not to know much of the world, or of the snares youth is exposed to; depend upon it, these are very bad women; I can see it by all their actions; and if thou art not upon thy guard, they will draw thee into some danger; they are strangers to thee, and I advise thee, in a friendly concern for thy welfare, to have no acquaintance with them."

"Indeed," said Benjamin, with much surprise, "I see nothing out of the way in them. They are intelligent and social; and I am rather surprised at your suspicions."

"But I have heard them say enough to convince me that my suspicions are well founded," replied the old lady; and she repeated to him some of their conversation which she had overheard.

"You are right, then," quickly answered Benjamin, after listening to her. "I am much obliged to you for your advice, and I will heed it."

Just before they arrived at New York, the young women invited him to call at their residence, naming the street and number, but he did not accept their invitation. The next day the captain missed a silver spoon and other things from the cabin, and suspecting the two girls, had their residence searched, where the missing articles were found, in consequence of which the artful thieves were punished. Benjamin always felt thankful to the old lady for her timely warning, and considered that following her advice probably saved him from trouble and ruin.

Collins had been in New York several days when Benjamin arrived. The latter was astounded to find him intoxicated when they met.

"Can it be," he exclaimed to Collins, "that you are intemperate?"

"I intemperate!" retorted Collins, disposed to resent the accusation. "Do you call me drunk?"

"No, you are not exactly drunk; but then you are disguised with liquor, and I am utterly astonished. Once you was as temperate and industrious as any young man in Boston, and far more respected than most of them. How did it happen that you formed this evil habit?"

Collins saw that he could not deceive Benjamin; so he made a clean breast of the matter, and confessed to have formed intemperate habits soon after Benjamin first left Boston. He said that his appetite for brandy was strong, and that he had been intoxicated every day since his arrival in New York.

"I have lost all my money," he said, "and have nothing to pay my bills."

"Lost your money!" exclaimed Benjamin. "How did you lose that?"

"I lost it by gaming," he replied.

"What! a gambler, too?"

"Yes, if you will have it so," answered Collins, somewhat coolly; "and you must lend me money to pay my bills."

"If I had known this," continued Benjamin, "I would not have persuaded you to leave Boston. And here let me tell you, that it is impossible for you to find a situation unless you reform."

"Perhaps so," answered Collins; "but that is not the question now that interests me. I want to know whether you will lend me money to pay my bills here and go on my journey?"

"I must, for aught I see," replied Benjamin. "I should not leave you here without money and friends, of course, for that would be cruel. But you must try to reform."

Collins was a very clever young man, as we have seen, possessing marked mathematical talents, and he might have become one of the first scholars of his day, had he enjoyed the advantages of a course of study. Some of the clergymen of Boston showed him much attention on account of his abilities and love of books. But strong drink blasted his hopes.

In New York, Benjamin received a message from Governor Burnet, inviting him to call at his house. This was quite as unexpected as the visit of Governor Keith, and he began to think that governors had a passionate regard for him. He found, however, that the Governor had learned from the captain of the sloop, that he had a young man on board who brought with him a large number of books from Boston. This interested the Governor, and was the occasion of his sending the aforesaid invitation to Benjamin.

He accepted the invitation, and would have taken Collins with him if the latter had been sober. Governor Burnet received him with much cordiality, showed him his large library, and conversed freely about books and authors for some time. It was an agreeable interview to Benjamin, the more so because it was the second time that a Governor had sought him out, and showed him attention.

They proceeded to Philadelphia. On the way Benjamin collected Vernon's debt, which proved fortunate, since otherwise his money would not have carried him through, from having had the bills of two to pay. A good trip brought them safely to their place of destination, and Collins boarded with Benjamin, at the latter's expense, waiting for an opening in some counting-room.

The reader may be curious to learn the fate of Collins, and we will briefly record it here. He tried to secure a situation, but his dram-drinking habits frustrated his exertions. Every few days he went to Benjamin for money, knowing that he had that of Vernon, always promising to pay as soon as he found business. Benjamin, in the kindness of his heart, lent him little by little, until he was troubled to know what he should do if Vernon should call for the money. Sometimes he lectured Collins severely for his habits, until their friendship was essentially modified. One day they were in a boat with other young men, on the Delaware, when Collins refused to row.

"We shall not row you," said Benjamin.

"You *will* row me, or stay all night on the water, just as you please," retorted Collins.

"We can stay as long as you can," continued Benjamin. "I shall not row you."

"Come, Ben, let us row," said one of the young men. "If he don't want to row let him sit still."

"Row him, if you wish to," replied Benjamin, "I shall not."

"Yes, you will," shouted Collins, starting from his seat. "I will be rowed home, and you shall help do it, or I will throw you overboard;" and he hurried to execute his threat. But, as he came up and struck at him, Benjamin clapped his head under his thighs, and rising, threw him head over heels into the river. He knew that Collins was a good swimmer, so that he had no fears about his drowning.

"Will you row now?" he inquired, as Collins swam towards the boat.

"Not a stroke," he answered, angrily; whereupon they sent the boat forward out of his reach, with one or two strokes of the oar. Again and again they allowed him to approach the boat, when they repeated the question: "Will you promise to row?" and as often received an emphatic "No" for a reply. At length, perceiving that he was quite exhausted, they drew him in without extorting from him a promise to row.

This scene closed the intimate relations of Benjamin and Collins. They scarcely spoke together civilly afterward. Collins sailed for Barbadoes within a few weeks after, and he was never heard from again. He probably died there, a miserable sot, and Benjamin lost all the money he lent him. In later life, Benjamin Franklin referred to this event, and spoke of himself as having received retribution for his influence over Collins. For, when they were so intimate in Boston, Benjamin corrupted his religious opinions by advocating doubts about the reality of religion, until Collins became a thorough sceptic. Until that time he was industrious, temperate, and honest. But having lost his respect for religion, he was left without restraint, and went rapidly to ruin. Benjamin was the greatest sufferer by his fall, and thus was rebuked for influencing him to treat religion with contempt.

Benjamin immediately sought an interview with Governor Keith, and told him the result of his visit home, and gave his father's reasons for declining to assist him.

"But since he will not set you up," said the Governor, "I will do it myself. Give me an inventory of the things necessary to be had from England, and I will send for them. You shall repay me when you are able; I am resolved to have a good printer here, and I am sure you must succeed."

This was said with such apparent cordiality that Benjamin did not doubt that he meant just what he affirmed, so he yielded to his suggestion to make out an inventory of necessary articles. In the meantime he went to work for Keimer.

CHAPTER XX.

A LITERARY GAME.

AT this point it is necessary to speak of Benjamin's associates. He was not long in finding new acquaintances in Philadelphia. His industry and general good habits won the respect and confidence of all who came in contact with him. Among those who particularly pleased him were three young men, Charles Osborne, Joseph Watson, and James Ralph, all lovers of reading. Their literary tendencies no doubt attracted Benjamin, and caused him to value their companionship more highly. The first two were clerks of Charles Brockden, an eminent conveyancer of the town, and the other was a merchant's clerk. Watson was a pious young man of sterling integrity, while the others were more lax in their religious opinions and principles. All were sensible young men, much above the average of this class in intellectual endowments. Osborne and Ralph were imaginative and poetical, and frequently tried their talents at verse-making.

Much of their leisure time was spent together, reading to each other, and discussing what they read. Even their Sundays were often wickedly devoted to such intellectual pastime on the banks of the Schuylkill, whither they strolled, instead of visiting the house of God—all except Watson, who had too much religious principle thus to desecrate the Sabbath.

"You overrate your talent for poetry," said Osborne to Ralph, at one of their interviews. "You will never make a poet, if you live to be as old as Methuselah."

"Much obliged for your compliment," answered Ralph; "but it does not alter my own opinion. All poets have their faults when they begin. It is practice that makes perfect."

"It will take something more than practice to make a poet of you," continued Osborne. "That piece which you have just read has no poetry about it. Besides, if you should become a poet, it will not bring you a fortune, as you seem to think."

"Perhaps not; but I am confident that a poet may easily win both popularity and a livelihood. At any rate, I am determined to try it, in spite of your decidedly poor opinion of my abilities."

"Well, I advise you to stick to the business to which you were bred," added Osborne, "if you would keep out of the poor-house. A good clerk is better than a bad poet"—and he cast a particularly roguish glance at Ralph as he said it.

"You need not set yourself up for a critic," said Benjamin to Osborne, after hearing these remarks. "I think more of Ralph as a poet than I do of you as a critic. You are not willing to grant that his productions have any merit at all; but I think they have. Moreover, it is a good practice for him to write poetry, to improve himself in the use of language."

"Fiddlestick!" retorted Osborne; "it is wasting his time, that might be profitably employed in reading."

"Not half so much as your empty criticisms are wasting your breath," said Benjamin, with a smile. "But, look here, I will tell you what we better do. At our next meeting each one of us shall bring a piece of poetry, of our own making, and we will compare notes, and criticise each other."

"I will agree to that," replied Ralph.

"And so will I," added Osborne, "provided you will decide upon the subject now, so that all shall have fair play."

"We will do that, of course," answered Benjamin. "Have you a subject to suggest?"

"None, unless it is a paraphrase of the eighteenth Psalm, which describes the descent of the Deity."

"A capital subject," said Benjamin; "what do you say to taking that, Ralph?"

"I am satisfied with it," replied Ralph; "and more, too,—I rather like it."

Thus it was agreed that each one should write a poetical paraphrase of the eighteenth Psalm for their next meeting, and with this understanding they separated.

Just before the time of their next meeting, Ralph called upon Benjamin with his piece, and asked him to examine it.

"I have been so busy," said Benjamin, "that I have not been able to write anything, and I shall be obliged to appear unprepared. But I should like to read yours;" and he proceeded to examine it.

"That is excellent," said he, after reading it. "You have not written anything that is equal to this."

"But," said Ralph, "Osborne never will allow the least merit in anything of mine, but makes a thousand criticisms, out of mere envy. He will do so with that piece, I have no doubt."

"If he does, it will prove that he is prejudiced against you, or is no judge of poetry," replied Benjamin.

"I have a plan to test him," continued Ralph. "He is not so jealous of you; I wish, therefore, you would take this piece and produce it as yours. I will make some excuse and have nothing. We shall then hear what he will say to it."

"I will do it," answered Benjamin, who was well convinced that Osborne was prejudiced against Ralph; "but I must transcribe it, so that it will appear in my own handwriting."

"Certainly; and be careful that you don't let the secret out."

They met at the appointed time. Watson was the first to read his performance. Osborne came next, and his piece was much better than Watson's. Ralph noticed two or three blemishes, but pointed out many beauties in it.

"I have nothing to read," said Ralph, whose turn came next in order. "I will try to do my part next time."

"Poets ought to be ready at any time," remarked Osborne jestingly. "Well, then, Ben, let us have yours."

"I rather think I must be excused," answered Benjamin, feigning an unwillingness to read.

"No excuse for you," said Osborne. "You have it written, for I saw it in your hand."

"That is true," replied Benjamin; "but after such fine productions as we have heard, there is little encouragement for me to read this. I think I must correct it and dress it up a little before I read it."

"Not a word of it," said Ralph. "There is no excuse for any one who is prepared."

So, after much urging, Benjamin proceeded to read the verses, with seeming diffidence, all listening with rapt attention.

"You must read that again," said Osborne, when the first reading was finished; which Benjamin consented to do.

"You surprise me, Ben," said Osborne, after the piece was read the second time. "You are a genuine poet. I had no idea that you could write like that."

"Nor I," added Watson. "It is better than half the poetry that is printed. If we had not given out the subject, I should have charged you with stealing it."

"What do *you* say, Ralph?" inquired Osborne. "You are a poet, and ought to be a judge of such matters."

"I don't think it is entirely faultless," responded Ralph. "You have commended it full as highly as it will bear, in my estimation."

"Well done!" exclaimed Osborne. "Your opinion of that piece proves that you are destitute of poetical taste, as I have told you before."

Ralph and Benjamin saw that Osborne was fairly caught, and they hardly dared to exchange glances, lest they should betray themselves. They succeeded, however, in controlling themselves, and allowed Osborne to express himself most emphatically.

Ralph walked home with Osborne, and their conversation was upon Benjamin's poetry.

"Who would have imagined," said Osborne, "that Franklin was capable of such a performance,—such painting, such force, such fire! In common conversation he seems to have no choice of words; he hesitates and blunders; and yet, how he writes!"

"Possibly he may not have written it," suggested Ralph.

"That is the 'unkindest cut of all,'" retorted Osborne, "to charge him of plagiarism. Franklin would not descend to so mean a thing."

They parted for that night; but Ralph embraced the first opportunity to call on Benjamin, and have a sort of rejoicing over the success of their enterprise. They laughed to their hearts' content, and discussed the point of revealing the secret. They agreed that the real author of the article should be known at their next meeting.

Accordingly, the affair was so managed as to bring the facts of the case before their companions at their next gathering. Osborne was utterly confounded when the revelation was made, and knew not what to say for himself. Watson shook his whole frame with convulsive laughter at poor Osborne's expense, and Benjamin joined him with a keen relish. Never was a fellow in more mortifying predicament than this would-be critic, since it was now so manifest that he had been influenced by blind prejudice in his criticisms upon Ralph's poetry. It was certain now that he had given it his most emphatic indorsement. While Osborne was brought to confusion and suffered deservedly, the trick played upon him is not one which can be approved by right-thinking persons. Deceit is never commendable.

A few years after, Watson died in Benjamin's arms, much lamented by all his companions, who regarded him as "the best of their set." Osborne removed to the West Indies, where he became an eminent lawyer, but was early cut off by death. Of the others we shall have occasion to speak hereafter.

It is quite evident that this literary way of spending their leisure time was of great advantage to this group of youths. Doubtless it led to the cultivation of that taste which most of them who lived exhibited for literature and science in after life. It is certainly an example of the wise use of spare moments which the young may safely imitate.

CHAPTER XXI.

GOING TO ENGLAND.

AT the earliest opportunity, Benjamin presented the Governor with an inventory of the articles necessary in setting up the printing business.

"And what will be the probable expense of all these?" inquired the Governor.

"About one hundred pounds sterling, as nearly as I can estimate," he replied.

"But would it not prove an advantage for you to be there yourself, to select the types, and see that everything is good?"

"I suppose it would, though such a thing as going to England is scarcely possible with me."

"That remains to be seen," continued Governor Keith. "Another advantage of your being there is, that you could form acquaintances, and establish correspondence in the bookselling and stationery line."

"That would certainly be an advantage," replied Benjamin.

"Then get yourself ready to go in the Annis," said the Governor. The Annis was the annual ship that sailed between Philadelphia and London, and the only one, at that time, which performed this voyage. Instead of there being scores of vessels sailing between these two ports, as now, there was only this solitary one, going and returning once a year.

"It is not necessary to prepare immediately," answered Benjamin, "since it is several months before the Annis will sail."

"True; I only meant that you should be in readiness when the ship sails. It will be necessary for you still to keep the matter secret while you continue to work for Keimer."

Keimer, for whom Benjamin worked, was a singular man in some respects, and liked to draw him into discussions upon religious subjects. At one time he thought seriously of originating a new sect, and proposed to Benjamin to join him, as his masterly powers of argumentation would confound opponents. He wore his beard long, because it is somewhere said in the Mosaic Law, "*Thou shalt not mar the corners of thy beard.*" Also, he kept the seventh, instead of the first day of the week, as a Sabbath. Benjamin opposed him on these points, and their discussions were frequent and warm. Keimer often exhorted him to embrace his own peculiar views on these subjects. Finally, Benjamin replied, "I will do it, provided you will join me in not eating animal food, and I will adhere to them as long as you will stick to a vegetable diet."

Benjamin was here aiming at some diversion, since Keimer was a great eater, and thought much of a savoury dish. Benjamin wanted to starve him a little, as he thought some of his preaching and practice did not correspond.

"I should die," said Keimer, "if I adopt such a diet; my constitution will not bear it."

"Nonsense!" answered Benjamin. "You will be better than you are now. So much animal food is bad for any one."

"What is there left to eat when meat is taken away?" inquired Keimer. "Little or nothing, I should think."

"I will pledge myself to furnish recipes for forty palatable dishes," answered Benjamin, "and not one of them shall smell of the flesh-pots of Egypt."

"Who will prepare them? I am sure no woman in this town can do it."

"Each dish is so simple that any woman can easily prepare it," added Benjamin.

Keimer finally accepted the proposition. He was to become a vegetarian, and Benjamin was to embrace formally the long-beard doctrine, and observe the seventh day for a Sabbath. A woman was engaged to prepare their food and bring it to them, and Benjamin furnished her with a list of forty dishes, "in which there entered neither fish, flesh, nor fowl." For about three months Keimer adhered to this way of living, though it was very trying to him all the while. Benjamin was often diverted to see his manifest longings for fowl and flesh, and expected that he would soon let him off from keeping the seventh day and advocating long beards. At the end of three months, Keimer declared that he could hold out no longer, and the agreement was broken. It was a happy day for him; and to show his gladness, he ordered a roast pig, and invited Benjamin and two ladies to dine with him. But the pig being set upon the table before his guests arrived, the temptation was so great that he could not resist, and he devoured the whole of it before they came, thus proving that he was a greater pig than the one he swallowed.

It should be remarked here, that for some time Benjamin had not followed the vegetable diet which he adopted in Boston. The circumstances and reason of his leaving are thus given by himself:—

"In my first voyage from Boston to Philadelphia, being becalmed off Block Island, our crew employed themselves in catching cod, and hauled up a great number. Till then, I had stuck to my resolution to eat nothing that had had life; and on this occasion I considered, according to my master Tryon, the taking every fish as a kind of unprovoked murder, since none of them had nor could do us any injury that might justify this massacre. All this seemed very reasonable. But I had been formerly a great lover of fish, and when it came out of the frying-pan, it smelt admirably well. I balanced some time between principle and inclination, till recollecting that, when the fish were opened, I saw smaller fish taken out of their stomachs; then, thought I, 'If you eat one another, I don't see why we may not eat you.' So I dined upon cod very heartily, and have since continued to eat as other people; returning only now and then to a vegetable diet. So convenient a thing it is to be a *reasonable creature*, since it enables one to find or make a *reason* for everything one has a mind to do."

The time was now approaching for the Annis to sail, and Benjamin began to realize the trial of leaving his friends. A new tie now bound him to Philadelphia. A mutual affection existed between Miss Read and himself, and it had ripened into sincere and ardent love. He desired a formal engagement with her before his departure, but her mother interposed.

"Both of you are too young," said she,—"only eighteen! You cannot tell what changes may occur before you are old enough to be married."

"But that need not have anything to do with an engagement," said Benjamin. "We only pledge ourselves to marry each other at some future time."

"And why do you deem such a pledge necessary?" asked the good mother.

"Simply because 'a bird in the hand is worth two in the bush,'" replied Benjamin, with his face all wreathed with smiles.

"But I have not quite satisfied myself that it is best to give up my daughter to a printer," added Mrs. Read.

"How so?" asked Benjamin, with some anxiety.

"Because," she replied, "there are already several printing-offices in the country, and I doubt whether another can be supported."

"If I cannot support her by the printing business," answered Benjamin, "then I will do it some other way."

"I have no doubt of your good intentions; but you may not realize the fulfilment of all your hopes. I think you had better leave the matter as it is until you return from England, and see how you are prospered."

The old lady won the day, and the young couple agreed to proceed no further at present.

The above reference to the fact that only four or five printing-offices existed in America at that time, may serve to exhibit its rapid growth. For in 1840, there were *one thousand five hundred and fifty-seven* of them, and now probably there are twice that number.

"I am going to England with you, Benjamin," said Ralph one day, as they met. "Don't you believe it?"

"It is almost too good news to believe," replied Benjamin. "But I should be glad of your company, I assure you."

"It is true," continued Ralph. "I was not jesting when I told you, the other day, that I meant to go if I could."

"Then you are really in earnest? You mean to go?"

"To be sure I do. I have fully decided to go."

Benjamin did not ask him what he was going for; but, from some remarks he heard him make previously, he inferred that he was going out to establish a correspondence, and obtain goods to sell on commission. Nor did he learn to the contrary until after they arrived in London, when Ralph informed him that he did not intend to return,—that he had experienced some trouble with his wife's relations, and he was going away to escape from it, leaving his wife and child to be cared for by her friends.

As the time of their departure drew near, Benjamin called upon the Governor for letters of introduction and credit, which he had promised, but they were not ready. He called again, and they were still unwritten. At last, just as he was leaving, he called at his door, and his secretary, Dr. Baird, came out, and said: "The Governor is engaged upon important business now, but he will be at Newcastle before the Annis reaches there, and will deliver the letters to you there."

As soon as they reached Newcastle, Benjamin went to the Governor's lodgings for the letters, but was told by his secretary that he was engaged, and should be under the necessity of sending the letters to him on board the ship, before she weighed anchor. Benjamin was somewhat puzzled by this unexpected turn of affairs, but still he did not dream of deception or dishonesty. He returned to the vessel, and awaited her departure. Soon after her canvas was flung to the breeze, he went to the captain and inquired for the letters.

"I understand," said he, "that Colonel French brought letters on board from the Governor. I suppose some of them are directed to my care."

"Yes," replied the captain, "Colonel French brought a parcel of letters on board, and they were all put into the bag with others, so that I cannot tell whether any of them are for you or not. But you shall have an opportunity, before we reach England, of looking them over for yourself."

"I thank you," answered Benjamin; "that will be all that is necessary;" and he yielded himself up to enjoyment for the remainder of the voyage, without the least suspicion of disappointment and trouble.

When they entered the English Channel, the captain, true to his promise, allowed Benjamin to examine the bag of letters. He found several on which his name was written, as under his care, and some others he judged, from the handwriting, came from the Governor. One of them was addressed to Baskett, the King's printer, and another to a stationer, and these two, Benjamin was confident, were for him to take. In all he took seven or eight from the bag.

They arrived in London on the 24th of December, 1724, when Benjamin lacked about a month of being nineteen years old. Soon after he landed, he called upon the stationer to whom one of the letters was directed: "A letter, sir, from Governor Keith, of Pennsylvania, America!"

"I don't know such a person," replied the stationer, at the same time receiving the letter.

"O, this is from Riddlesden!" said he, on opening it. "I have lately found him to be a complete rascal, and I will have nothing to do with him, nor receive any letters from him;" and he handed back the letter to Benjamin, turned upon his heel, and left to wait upon a customer.

Benjamin was astonished and mortified. He had not the least suspicion that he was bearing any other than the Governor's letter, and he was almost bewildered for a moment. The thought flashed into his mind that the Governor had deceived him. In a few moments his thoughts brought together the acts of the Governor in the matter, and now he could see clearly evidence of insincerity and duplicity. He immediately sought out Mr. Denham, a merchant, who came over in the Annis with him, and gave him a history of the affair.

"Governor Keith is a notorious deceiver," said Mr. Denham. "I do not think he wrote a single letter for you, nor intended to do it. He has been deceiving you from beginning to end."

"He pretended to have many acquaintances here," added Benjamin, "to whom he promised to give me letters of credit, and I supposed that they would render me valuable assistance."

"Letters of credit!" exclaimed Denham. "It is a ludicrous idea. How could he write letters of credit, when he has no credit of his own to give? No one who knows him has the least confidence in his character. There is no dependence to be placed upon him in anything. He is entirely irresponsible."

"What, then, shall I do?" asked Benjamin with evident concern. "Here I am among strangers without the means of returning, and what shall I do?"

"I advise you to get employment in a printing-office here for the present. Among the printers here you will improve yourself, and, when you return to America, you will set up to greater advantage."

There was no alternative left for Benjamin but to find work where he could, and make the best of it. Again he had "paid too dear for the whistle," and must suffer for it. He took lodgings with Ralph in Little Britain, at three shillings and sixpence a week, and very soon obtained work at Palmer's famous printing-house in Bartholomew Close, where he laboured nearly a year. Ralph was not so successful in getting a situation. He made application here and there, but in vain; and, after several weeks of fruitless attempts at securing a place, he decided to leave London, and teach a country school. Previously, however, in company with Benjamin, he spent much time at plays and public amusements. This was rather strange, since neither of them had been wont to waste their time and money in this way; and years after, Benjamin spoke of it as a great error of his life, which he deeply regretted. But Ralph's departure put an end to this objectionable pleasure-seeking, and Benjamin returned to his studious habits when out of the office.

At this time, the ability to compose which he had carefully nurtured proved of great assistance to him. He was employed in the printing of Wollaston's "Religion of Nature," when he took exceptions to some of his reasoning, and wrote a dissertation thereon, and printed it, with the title, "A DISSERTATION ON LIBERTY AND NECESSITY, PLEASURE AND PAIN." This pamphlet fell into the hands of one Lyons, a surgeon, author of a book entitled "The Infallibility of Human Judgment," and he was so much pleased with it, that he sought out the author, and showed him marked attention. He introduced him to Dr. Mandeville, author of the "Fable of the Bees," and to Dr. Pemberton, who promised to take him to see Sir Isaac Newton. Sir Hans Sloane invited him to his house in Bloomsbury Square, and showed him all his curiosities. In this way, the small pamphlet which he wrote introduced him to distinguished men, which was of much advantage to him.

While he lodged in Little Britain, he made the acquaintance of a bookseller, by the name of Wilcox, who had a very large collection of secondhand books. Benjamin wanted to gain access to them, but he could not command the means to purchase; so he hit upon this plan: he proposed to Wilcox to pay him a certain sum per book for as many as he might choose to take out, read, and return, and Wilcox accepted his offer. In this transaction was involved the principle of the modern circulating library. It was the first instance of lending books on record, and for that reason becomes an interesting fact. It was another of the influences that served to send him forward in a career of honour and fame.

When he first entered the printing-house in London, he did press-work. There were fifty workmen in the establishment, and all of them but Benjamin were great beer-drinkers; yet he could lift more, and endure more fatigue, than any of them. His companion at the press was a notorious drinker, and consumed daily "a pint of beer before breakfast, a pint at breakfast with his food, a pint between breakfast and dinner, a pint at dinner, a pint in the afternoon about six o'clock, and another when he had done his day's work,"—in all six pints per day. They had an alehouse boy always in attendance upon the workmen.

"A detestable habit," said Benjamin to his fellow-pressman, "and a very expensive one, too."

"I couldn't endure the wear and tear of this hard work without it," replied the toper.

"You could accomplish more work, and perform it better, by drinking nothing but cold water," rejoined Benjamin. "There is nothing like it to make one strong and healthy."

"Fudge! It may do for a Water-American like you, but Englishmen would become as weak as babes without it."

"That is false," said Benjamin. "With all your drinking *strong* beer in this establishment, you are the weakest set of workmen I ever saw. I have seen *you* tug away to carry a single form of type up and down stairs, when I always carry two. Your beer may be *strong*, but it makes you *weak*."

"You Americans are odd fellows, I confess," added the beer-swigger; "and you stick to your opinions like a tick."

"But look here, my good fellow," continued Benjamin. "Do you not see that the bodily strength afforded by beer can be only in proportion to the grain or flour of the barley dissolved in the water of which it is made?

There must be more flour in a pennyworth of bread than there is in a whole quart of beer; therefore, if you eat that with a pint of water, it will give you more strength than two or three pints of beer. Is it not so?"

The man was obliged to acknowledge that it appeared to be so.

Benjamin continued: "You see that I am supplied with a large porringer of hot water-gruel, sprinkled with pepper, crumbled with bread, and a bit of butter in it, for just the price of a pint of beer, three-halfpence. Now, honestly, is not this much better for me, and for you, than the same amount of beer?"

Thus Benjamin thorned his companions with arguments against the prevailing habit of beer-drinking. Gradually he acquired an influence over many of them, by precept and example, and finally they abandoned their old habit, and followed his better way of living. He wrought a thorough reformation in the printing-office; and the fact shows what one young man can do in a good cause, if he will but set his face resolutely in that direction. Benjamin possessed the firmness, independence, and moral courage to carry out his principles,—just the thing which many a youth of his age lack, and consequently make shipwreck of their hopes.

The only amusement which Benjamin seems to have enjoyed as much as he did literary recreation, was swimming. From his boyhood he delighted to be in the water, performing wonderful feats, and trying his skill in various ways. At one time he let up his kite, and, taking the string in his hand, lay upon his back on the top of the water, when the kite drew him a mile in a very agreeable manner. At another time he lay floating upon his back and slept for an hour by the watch. The skill which he had thus acquired in the art of swimming won him a reputation in England. On several occasions he exhibited his remarkable attainments of this kind, and the result was that he was applied to by Sir William Wyndham to teach his two sons to swim. Some advised him to open a swimming-school, and make it his profession; but he very wisely concluded to leave the water to the fish, and confine himself to the land.

Benjamin had been in London nearly eighteen months, when Mr. Denham, the merchant of whom we have spoken, proposed to him to return to Philadelphia, and act in the capacity of bookkeeper for him, and offered him fifty pounds a year, with the promise to promote him, and finally establish him in business. Benjamin had a high respect for Mr. Denham, and the new field of labour appeared to him inviting, so that he accepted the proposition with little hesitation, and made preparations to leave England, quitting for ever, as he thought, the art of printing, which he had thoroughly learned.

Forty years after Benjamin worked in Palmer's printing-office, he visited England in the service of his country, widely known as a sagacious statesman and profound philosopher. He took occasion to visit the old office where he once laboured with the beer-drinkers, and, stepping up to the press on which he worked month after month, he said: "Come, my friends, we will drink together. It is now forty years since I worked, like you, at this press, as a journeyman printer." With these words, he sent out for a gallon of porter, and they drank together according to the custom of the times. That press, on which he worked in London, is now in the Patent-office at Washington.

CHAPTER XXII.

FAREWELL TO ENGLAND.

ON the 23rd day of July, 1726, Benjamin sailed for Philadelphia, in company with Mr. Denham. After a successful and rather pleasant voyage of nearly three months, they reached Philadelphia, much to the satisfaction of Benjamin, who always enjoyed his stay there. He was now twenty years of age.

"Ah! is it you, Benjamin? I am glad to see you back again," said Keimer, as his old journeyman made his appearance; and he shook his hand as if his heart was in it. "I began to think you had forsaken us."

"Not yet," replied Benjamin. "I think too much of Philadelphia to forsake it yet."

"Want work at your old business, I suppose?" added Keimer. "I have a plenty of it. You see I have improved things since you were here; my shop is well supplied with stationery, plenty of new types, and a good business!"

"I see that you have made considerable advance," replied Benjamin. "I am glad that you prosper."

"And I shall be glad to employ you, as none of my men are complete masters of the business."

"But I have relinquished my old trade," answered Benjamin. "I——"

"Given up the printing business!" interrupted Keimer. "Why is that?"

"I have made arrangements with Mr. Denham to keep his books, and serve him generally in the capacity of clerk."

"I am sorry for that, and I think you will be eventually. It is a very uncertain business."

"Well, I have undertaken it for better or worse," said Benjamin, as he rose to leave the shop.

As he was going down the street, who should he meet but Governor Keith, who had been removed from his office, and was now only a common citizen. The ex-Governor appeared both surprised and ashamed at seeing him, and passed by him without speaking.

Benjamin was quite ashamed to meet Miss Read, since he had not been true to his promise. Though he had been absent eighteen months, he had written her but a single letter, and that was penned soon after his arrival in

London, to inform her that he should not return at present. His long absence and silence convinced her that he had ceased to regard her with affection; in consequence of which, at the earnest persuasion of her parents, she married a potter by the name of Rogers. He turned out to be a miserable fellow, and she lived with him only a short time. He incurred heavy debts; ran away to the West Indies to escape from his creditors, and there died.

Miss Read (she refused to bear the name of Rogers) was disconsolate and sad, and Benjamin pitied her sincerely, inasmuch as he considered himself to blame in the matter. He was not disposed to shield himself from the censure of the family, had they been disposed to administer any; but the old lady took all the blame upon herself, because she prevented an engagement, and persuaded her daughter to marry Rogers.

These circumstances rendered his meeting with Miss Read less unpleasant, so far as his own want of fidelity was concerned. His intimacy with the family was renewed, and they frequently invited him there to tea, and often sought his advice on business of importance.

Mr. Denham opened a store in Water Street, and Benjamin entered upon his new business with high hopes. He made rapid progress in acquiring knowledge of traffic, and soon became expert in keeping accounts and selling goods. But in February, 1727, when Benjamin was twenty-one years of age, both he and his employer were prostrated by sickness. Benjamin's disease was pleurisy, and his life was despaired of, though he unexpectedly recovered. Mr. Denham lingered along for some time, and died. His decease was the occasion of closing the store and throwing Benjamin out of business. It was a sad disappointment, but not wholly unlike the previous checkered experience of his life. He had become used to "ups and downs."

As a token of his confidence and esteem, Mr. Denham left a small legacy to Benjamin,—a fact that speaks well for the young man's faithfulness. And here it should be said, that, whatever faults the hero of our story had, he always served his employers with such ability and fidelity as won their approbation and confidence. Unlike many youth, who care not for their employers' interests if they but receive their wages and keep their places, he ever did the best he could for those who employed him. He proved himself trustworthy and efficient; and here is found one secret of his success.

In his disappointment, Benjamin sought the advice of his brother-in-law, Captain Homes, who happened to be in Philadelphia at the time.

"I advise you to return to your old business," said he. "I suppose you can readily get work here, can you not?"

"All I want," Benjamin answered. "Keimer was very anxious to employ me when I returned from England, and I dare say that he would hire me now."

"Then I would close a bargain with him at once, were I in your place. I think you will succeed better at your trade than in any other business, and perhaps the way will soon be prepared for you to open a printing-office of your own."

This advice was followed without delay, and Keimer was eager to employ him. At the outset, he offered him extra wages to take the entire management of his printing-office, so that he (Keimer) might attend more closely to his stationer's shop. The offer was accepted, and Benjamin commenced his duties immediately. He soon found, however, that Keimer's design in offering him so large wages was, that the hands he already employed might be improved under his experience, when it would not be necessary for him to hire so competent a person. The facts show us that good workmen can command employment and high wages, when poor ones are obliged to beg their bread.

Among Keimer's workmen was an Oxford student, whose time he had bought for four years. He was about eighteen years of age, smart and intelligent. Benjamin very naturally became interested in him, as it was quite unusual to find an Oxford scholar acting in the capacity of a bought servant; and he received from him the following brief account of his life. He "was born in Gloucester, educated at a grammar-school, and had been distinguished among the scholars for some apparent superiority in performing his part when they exhibited plays; belonged to the Wits' Club there, and had written some pieces in prose and verse, which were printed in the Gloucester newspapers. Thence was sent to Oxford, where he continued about a year, but not well satisfied; wishing, of all things, to see London, and become a player. At length, receiving his quarterly allowance of fifteen guineas, instead of discharging his debts, he went out of town, hid his gown in a furze-bush, and walked to London; where, having no friend to advise him, he fell into bad company, soon spent his guineas, found no means of being introduced among the players, grew necessitous, pawned his clothes, and wanted bread. Walking the street, very hungry, not knowing what to do with himself, a crimp's bill was put into his hand, offering immediate entertainment and encouragement to such as would bind themselves to work in America. He went directly, signed the indentures, was put into the ship, and came over; never writing a line to his friends, to acquaint them what was become of him."

Such a case has several important lessons for the young. In the first place, it shows the danger that attends theatrical performances. Youth often wonder that good people object to them; but here they may see one reason of their opposition. It was at the school in Oxford that he imbibed a love for the stage. There he participated in dramatic plays, which caused him to run away, and seek a residence in London, where he was ruined. There are hundreds of similar examples, and these cause good people to condemn theatrical amusements. It is said that when Lord Jeffrey was a youth, at the college in Glasgow, he was instrumental in originating a dramatic performance. The play was selected, and a room of the college designated as a fitting theatre, when the authorities interfered, and forbade them to perform the play. Their interference aroused the ire of Jeffrey, who, in his "Notes on Lectures," denounced their conduct as "the meanest, most illiberal, and despicable." Many youth cherish similar feelings towards those who condemn such performances; and, if one of the number shall read these pages, we would point him to the sad end of the Oxford student.

This case also illustrates the sad consequences of keeping bad company, as well as the perils of the city. He associated with the vicious in London, and became really a vagabond in consequence.

As the workmen improved under Benjamin's supervision, Keimer evidently began to think of discharging him, or cutting down his wages. On paying his second quarter's wages, he told him that he could not continue to pay him so much. He became less civil, frequently found fault, and plainly tried to make Benjamin's stay uncomfortable so that he would leave. At length a rare opportunity offered for him to make trouble. An unusual noise in the street one day caused Benjamin to put his head out of the window to see what was the matter. Keimer happened to be in the street, and seeing him, he cried out, "Put your head in, and attend to your business;" and added some reproachful words which all in the street heard. Then, hastening up into the office, he continued his insulting language.

"Men who work for me must give better heed to their business," said he. "If they care more for a noise in the street than for their work, it is time they left."

"I am ready to leave any time you please," retorted Benjamin, who was considerably nettled by such treatment. "I am not dependent on you for a living, and I shall not be treated in this way long, I assure you."

"That, indeed!" exclaimed Keimer. "You would not stay another hour if it were not for our agreement, in accordance with which I now warn you that, at the end of a quarter's time, I shall hire you no more."

"You need not regret that you cannot send me away to-day," answered Benjamin. "I shall work no longer for a man who will treat me thus;" and, taking his hat, he left. As he passed down, he requested Meredith, one of the hands, to bring some things which he left behind to his lodgings.

In the evening Meredith went to see Benjamin, carrying the articles referred to.

"What shall you do now?" Meredith inquired.

"I shall return to Boston forthwith."

"I wouldn't do that. You can do much better here than you can there."

"What can I do here now?"

"Set up business for yourself."

"I have no money to do it with."

"My father has," said Meredith; "and I will go into company with you if he will furnish the means. I am not acquainted with the business, and you are; so I will furnish the capital, and you shall manage the concern, and we will share the profits equally."

"Your father will never do it," suggested Benjamin.

"I am confident that he will," replied Meredith. "He has a high opinion of you, and he wants a good opportunity to set me up. I will ask him, at any rate."

"I would like such an enterprise myself," added Benjamin; "but can we succeed against Keimer? He will now do all he can to crush me."

"He will be crushed himself before long," answered Meredith. "I happen to know that he is in debt for all the property in his hands. He keeps his shop miserably, too; often sells without profit in order to raise money; and trusts people without keeping accounts. He will fail as surely as he keeps on in this way."

"I will agree to your plan if you can make it work," said Benjamin. "See your father immediately, and let me know the result."

Accordingly, Meredith saw his father, and he was ready to furnish the necessary capital, because of his high regard for Benjamin.

"I am the more ready to do this," said he to Benjamin, afterwards, "because of your good influence over my son. You have prevailed upon him to leave off drinking to excess, and I hope he will be persuaded, by your more intimate connection in business, to reform entirely."

It was settled that they should set up business as soon as they could procure the necessary articles from England.

CHAPTER XXIII.

SETTING UP BUSINESS.

AGREEABLY to the arrangement with Meredith, Benjamin made out an inventory of articles, which were immediately ordered from England. In the mean time he expected to find work at Bradford's printing-office, but was disappointed. It was only a few days, however, before he received a very civil message from Keimer, in which he said, "that old friends should not part for a few words, the effect of sudden passion," and urged him to return. The fact was, he had a prospect of being employed to print some paper-money in New Jersey, which would require cuts and various types that Benjamin only could supply, and, therefore, he wanted to re-engage him. Benjamin was not quite inclined to accept the proposition at first, but Meredith urged him to do it, on the ground that he himself would become better acquainted with the business in consequence; he, therefore, agreed to return.

It was several months before the new types arrived from London, and Benjamin continued in Keimer's service. Most of the time he spent with his employer at Burlington, executing the paper-money, and there made many friends, among whom was Judge Allen, the Secretary of the Province, several members of the Assembly, and the Surveyor-General, all of whom were of service to him when he set up business for himself. They were much pleased with Benjamin's intelligence and fidelity, so that they frequently invited him to their houses, while the ignorance and rudeness of Keimer so disgusted them, that they took little notice of him.

"You are completely master of your business," said the Surveyor-General to him; "and success is before you."

"I have improved my opportunities," modestly replied Benjamin, "to become as well acquainted with my business as I could. This half way of doing things I do not like."

"I commenced business in a very humble way," continued the Surveyor-General, "without expecting to ever possess such an estate as I do now."

"What was your business?"

"I wheeled clay for the brick-makers, and had not the opportunity of going to school at all in my boyhood. I did not learn to write until I became of age. I acquired my knowledge of surveying when I carried a chain for surveyors, who were pleased with my desire to learn the business, and assisted me. By constant industry and close application, with a good deal of perseverance, I have succeeded in reaching the place where you now see me."

"That is all the way any one can work his way up to an honourable position," said Benjamin.

"True, very true, and I am glad to see that you understand it. I am confident that you will beat this man Keimer at the business, and make a fortune in it at Philadelphia, if you go on as you have begun."

This example of industry and perseverance was encouraging to Benjamin in his circumstances. It was exactly suited to confirm him in his very proper views of industry and fidelity.

Meredith and Benjamin settled with Keimer and left him just before their types arrived, without letting him into the secret of their plans. The first intimation he had of their intentions was the opening of their printing-office near the market.

Many people were taken by surprise, and most of them predicted a failure, since there were two printers established there already. Not long after they commenced, an elderly man, whose name was Samuel Mickle, happened to be passing just as Benjamin came out of his office.

"Are you the young man," said Mickle, "who has lately opened a new printing-house?"

"I am, sir."

"I am sorry for you," said he, "for it is an expensive undertaking, and you are throwing away your money."

"How so?"

"Because Philadelphia is degenerating, and half the people are now bankrupt, or nearly so, and how can they support so many printers?"

"But the appearance of Philadelphia," replied Benjamin, "indicates thrift. See how many buildings are going up, and how rents are rising every month. This does not look like going backward."

"These are among the very things that will ruin us," responded Mickle. "They are not evidence of prosperity, but of extravagance, that will bring disaster sooner or later."

In this strain, Mickle, who was one of those eccentric and unhappy men who always look upon the dark side of things, went on, until Benjamin really began to feel dismayed. But on the whole, he believed that the evidence of his own senses was to the contrary, and so he soon forgot the interview. Mickle continued to live there some years, refusing to buy a house because the town was going to ruin, and at last he purchased one for five times what he could have had it for at the time he talked to Benjamin.

In their printing-office, Franklin suspended the following lines, which he composed:—

"All ye who come this curious art to see,To handle anything must careful be;Lest by a slight touch, ere you are aware,You may do mischief which you can't repair,Lo! this advice we give to every stranger!Look on and welcome, but to touch there's danger."

This singular notice attracted some attention, and elicited remarks from different visitors.

In order to win the confidence of the public, and secure their patronage, Benjamin resolved at the outset to exhibit to all beholders several qualities which guarantee success; namely, industry, economy, integrity, and close application to his business. All of them had become habits with him, and hence it was easy for him to conduct in this manner.

In respect to industry, he laboured incessantly. Even some of his hours that ought to have been devoted to sleep were spent in his office at hard work.

Mention being made of the new printing-house at the "Merchants' Every-night Club," "It will prove a failure," said one.

"Of course it will," added another. "Two such young fellows cannot get business enough to support them, with two established printers here."

This was the general opinion. But Dr. Baird, who was present, said: "It will prove a success, for the industry of that Franklin is superior to anything I ever saw of the kind. I see him still at work when I go home from club, and he is at work again before his neighbours are out of bed."

This remark was appreciated by the members, and soon after one of them offered to supply the young printers with stationery, if they desired to open a shop.

It was his experience, doubtless, that caused him, years afterwards, to give the following advice to a "young tradesman:"—

> "The most trifling actions that affect a man's credit are to be regarded. The sound of your hammer at five in the morning, or nine at night, heard by a creditor, makes him easy six months longer; but if he sees you at a billiard-table, or hears your voice at a tavern, when you should be

at work, he sends for his money the next day; demands it, before he can receive it, in a lump."

He also wrote: "He that idly loses five shillings' worth of time loses five shillings, and might as prudently throw five shillings into the sea."

One fine morning, after Meredith and Franklin opened a stationer's shop and bookstore, a lounger stepped in, and, after looking over the articles, inquired of the boy in attendance the price of a certain book.

"One dollar," was the answer.

"One dollar," said the lounger, "can't you take less than that?"

"No indeed; one dollar is the price."

After waiting some time he asked: "Is Mr. Franklin at home?"

"Yes, he is in the printing-office."

"I want to see him," said the lounger.

The shop-boy soon informed Franklin (as we will henceforth call him) that a gentleman was waiting to see him in the shop.

"Mr. Franklin, what is the lowest you can take for this book?" he asked, as Franklin came in. At the same time he held up the book at which he had been looking.

"One dollar and a quarter," was the reply.

"One dollar and a quarter! Why, your young man asked but a dollar."

"True," said Franklin, "and I could have better afforded to take a dollar then, than to have been taken out of the office."

The lounger looked surprised, and rather concluded that Franklin was jesting, he said, "Come, now, tell me the lowest you can take for it."

"One dollar and a half."

"A dollar and a half? Why, you offered it yourself for one dollar and a quarter?"

"Yes," answered Franklin, "and I had better have taken that price then, than a dollar and a half now."

The lounger paid the price, and went out of the shop, feeling the severity of the rebuke. Such was the value he attached to his time.

Franklin always ascribed his industrious habits to the frequent counsels of his father on the subject, which were generally closed by repeating the text of Scripture, "Seest thou a man diligent in his calling, he shall stand before kings, he shall not stand before mean men,"—a prophecy that was singularly fulfilled in his own case, as we shall see hereafter, for he had the honour of standing before *five* kings, and even dined with the King of Denmark.

His economy was equal to his industry. He arrayed himself in the plainest manner, although he aimed to look neat and tidy. His board was simple and cheap, and everything about his business was graduated on the most economical principles. In order to save expense, and at the same time show the public that he was not proud, and above his business, he wheeled home the paper which he bought. This single act had its influence in gaining the public confidence. For when a young man gets above his business, he is quite sure to have a fall. Since Franklin's day, in the city of Richmond, a young man went to the market to purchase a turkey. He looked around for some one to carry it home for him, being too proud to do it himself, and finding no one, he began to fret and swear, much to the annoyance of bystanders. A gentleman stepped up to him and said, "That is in my way, and I will take your turkey home for you." When they came to the house, the young fop asked, "What shall I pay you?" "O, nothing at all," replied the gentleman, "it was all in the way, and it was no trouble to me." As he passed on, the young man turned to a person near by, and inquired, "Who is that polite old gentleman who brought home my turkey for me?" "O," replied he, "that was Judge Marshall, Chief Justice of the United States." "Why did *he* bring home my turkey?" "He did it to give you a rebuke, and teach you to attend to your own business," was the answer.

How contemptible does such a character appear in contrast with Franklin! It is not strange that the public withhold their confidence from the fop, and bestow it upon the industrious. Judge Marshall was a great man, and great men never get above their business. Franklin became a great man, and one reason of it was, that he never became too proud to wait upon himself.

After he married Miss Read, and commenced housekeeping, he still adhered to the same principle of economy. Instead of doing as many young men do at this era of life, living beyond their income, he continued frugal. He said of himself and wife, "We kept no idle servants, our table was plain and simple, our furniture of the cheapest. For instance, my breakfast was for a long time bread and milk (no tea), and I ate it out of a twopenny earthen porringer, with a pewter spoon." Thus he reduced to practice the couplet which he wrote:—

"Vessels large may venture more,But little boats should keep near shore."

And qualified himself to pen such maxims as the following:—

"It is easier to suppress the first desire, than to satisfy all that follow it."

"It is as truly folly for the poor to ape the rich, as for the frog to swell in order to equal the ox."

"Pride breakfasts with plenty, dines with poverty, and sups with infamy."

His integrity in transacting business was no less marked. Strict honesty characterized all his dealings with men. An exalted idea of justice pervaded his soul. His word of honour was as good as his note of hand. Even his disposition to castigate and censure in his writings, so manifest in Boston at seventeen years of age, and which his father rebuked, was overcome. After he set up a paper in Philadelphia, a gentleman handed him an article for its columns.

"I am very busy now," said Franklin, "and you will confer a favour by leaving it for my perusal at my leisure."

"That I will do," replied the writer "and call again to-morrow."

The next day the author called. "What is your opinion of my article?" he asked.

"Why, sir, I am sorry to say that I cannot publish it," answered Franklin.

"Why not? What is the matter with it?"

"It is highly scurrilous and defamatory," replied Franklin. "But being at a loss on account of my poverty, whether to reject it or not, I thought I would put it to this issue. At night, when my work was done, I bought a twopenny loaf, on which I supped heartily, and then, wrapping myself in my great coat, slept very soundly on the floor until morning, when another loaf and mug of water afforded a pleasant breakfast. Now, sir, since I can live very comfortably in this manner, why should I prostitute my press to personal hatred or party passion for a more luxurious living?"

Some writer has said that this incident of Franklin's early life is akin to Socrates's reply to King Archelaus, who pressed him to give up preaching in the dirty streets of Athens, and come and live with him in his costly palace: "*Meal, please your Majesty, is a halfpenny a peck at Athens, and water I get for nothing.*"

Their business prospered well; but Meredith's intemperate habits were so strong, that he was frequently seen intoxicated in the streets, which occasioned much gossip about town concerning the prospects of their success. To add to their embarrassment, Meredith's father was unable to meet the last payment of a hundred pounds upon the printing-house, and they were sued. But William Coleman and Robert Grace, two of Franklin's companions, came to his assistance.

"We will lend you the means to take the business into your own hands," said Coleman. "It is much to your discredit to be connected with Meredith, who is seen reeling through the streets so often."

"But I cannot honourably propose a dissolution of partnership," replied Franklin, "while there is any prospect that the Merediths will fulfil their part of the contract, because I feel myself under great obligations for what they have done."

"They will not be able to fulfil the contract," said Grace; "that is out of the question."

"That is my opinion," responded Franklin; "still, I must wait and see what they do. If they fail to meet their obligations, then I shall feel at liberty to act otherwise."

The matter was left here for some weeks, when Franklin said to Meredith, meaning to sound him on the matter of dissolving the partnership: "Perhaps your father is dissatisfied with the part you have undertaken in this affair of ours, and is unwilling to advance for you and I what he would for you alone. If that is the case, tell me, and I will resign the whole to you, and go about my business."

"Sawdust Pudding"—Anecdote of Franklin's Independence.—See page 242.

"No," he answered, "my father has really been disappointed, and is really unable; and I am unwilling to distress him further. I see this is a business I am unfit for. I was bred a farmer; and it was folly in me to come to town, and put myself, at thirty years of age, an apprentice to learn a new trade. Many of our Welsh people (he was a Welshman) are going to settle in North Carolina, where land is cheap. I am inclined to go with them, and follow my old employment; you may find friends to assist you. If you will take the debts of the company upon you, return to my father the hundred pounds he has advanced, pay my little personal debts, and give me thirty pounds and a new saddle, I will relinquish the partnership, and leave the whole in your hands."

Franklin accepted this proposition, and, with the aid of his two friends, was soon established in business alone. His patronage increased rapidly, and he was able to pay off his debts. In a very short time he commanded the chief printing business of the town, and Keimer sold out, and removed to Barbadoes. The *Pennsylvania Gazette*, which he commenced printing before Meredith left him, won the public favour, and became a source of profit. As an example of his resolution and firmness, and his economy and prudence, it is said that certain subscribers to his paper were incensed at an article that appeared in its columns, and they threatened to "stop their patronage;" whereupon Franklin invited them to dine with him, and, having set before them a coarse meal mixture, from which his guests drew back, he remarked: "Gentlemen, a man who can subsist on *sawdust pudding* need call no man *patron*."

Here, in early life, our hero laid the foundation of his fortune; and the reader need not be at a loss to discover the secret of his success. He made himself by the sterling elements of character which he cultivated.

CHAPTER XXIV.

THE JUNTO.

SOON after Franklin returned from England, he was instrumental in forming his literary associates into a club for mutual improvement, called the "JUNTO," which met every Friday evening. This club continued nearly forty years, and Franklin said of it, "It was the best school of philosophy, morality, and politics, that then existed in the Province; for our queries, which were read the week preceding their discussion, put us upon reading with attention on the several subjects, that we might speak more to the purpose; and here, too, we acquired better habits of conversation, everything being studied in our rules which might prevent our disgusting each other."

"I have a proposition to submit," said Franklin, at one of their meetings, "and it is this. We frequently have occasion to refer to our books, in our discussions, and I propose that we bring our books together in this room, and form a library; each having the privilege of using the books of the other."

"I like the plan much," said Parsons, one of the members. "Nobody but Franklin would have thought of it."

"I think that every member must subscribe to this measure," said Coleman. "I hope it will be done at once."

And thus it went round the room, each one expressing his approval of the plan. The consequence was, that one end of the room was filled with volumes; and the plan proved profitable to all.

At that time, books were very scarce. "There was not a good bookseller's shop in any of the Colonies to the southward of Boston." The readers of Pennsylvania usually sent to England for their books, which was both troublesome and expensive.

The members of the "JUNTO" derived so much benefit from the plan of bringing their books together, that Franklin conceived the idea of establishing a library, and formed his plan, which was successful. He found fifty persons in town, mostly young tradesmen, who were willing to pay down forty shillings each, and ten shillings per annum; and with these the library was commenced. This was the first library ever established in this country, and it now numbers more than sixty thousand volumes. Since that day libraries have multiplied rapidly.

The following are some of the questions for the "JUNTO," and they show that it was really a thorough and valuable organization.

"Have you met with anything, in the author you last read, remarkable, or suitable to be communicated to the Junto? particularly in history, morality, poetry, physics, travels, mechanic arts, or other parts of knowledge."

"Hath any citizen failed in business, and what have you heard of the cause?"

"Have you lately heard of any citizen's thriving well, and by what means?"

"Do you know of a fellow-citizen who has lately done a worthy action, deserving praise and imitation; or who has lately committed an error, proper for us to be warned against and avoid?"

"What unhappy effects of intemperance have you lately observed or heard?—of imprudence?—of passion?—or of any other vice or folly?"

"What happy effects of temperance?—of prudence?—of moderation?—or of any other virtue?"

"Do you think of anything at present in which the Junto may be serviceable to *mankind*, to their country, to their friends, or to themselves?"

"Hath any deserving stranger arrived in town since last meeting, that you have heard of?—and what have you heard or observed of his character or merits?—and whether, think you, it lies in the power of the Junto to oblige him, or encourage him as he deserves?"

"Do you know of any deserving young beginner lately set up, whom it lies in the power of the Junto any way to encourage?"

"Have you lately observed any defect in the laws of your country, of which it would be proper to move the Legislature for an amendment? or do you know of any beneficial law that is wanting?"

"Is there any man whose friendship you want, and which the Junto, or any of them, can procure for you?"

This is a sample of the questions asked at their meetings, and answered. It is not difficult to see the mind of Franklin in these inquiries, and many of them were evidently suggested by his own experience.

Some of the questions discussed by the members of the Junto were as follows:—

"Is *sound* an entity or body?"

"How may the phenomena of vapours be explained?"

"Can any one particular form of government suit all mankind?"

"Is the emission of paper money safe?"

"How may smoky chimneys be best cured?"

"Which is least criminal,—a *bad* action joined with a *good* intention, or a *good* action with a *bad* intention?"

There have been improvements in almost everything in modern times, but we doubt if there has been much improvement upon the "JUNTO" in literary organizations for the young. It is not surprising, that, of the original twelve members (the number was limited to twelve), two became surveyors-general; one the inventor of a quadrant; one a distinguished mechanic and influential man; and one "a merchant of great note and a provincial judge;" and all but one or two, respectable and honoured men.

At this time, Franklin had commenced the study of the languages, employing only such leisure moments as he had to master them. It was a great undertaking, but his application and perseverance were equal to the task. He began with French, and was soon able to read books in that language. Then he took Italian. A friend, who was studying it also, tempted him to play chess. He played a little, and finding that it consumed time, he refused to play any more, unless on the condition that "the victor in every game should have a right to impose a task, either of parts of the grammar to be got by heart, or in translations, which task the vanquished was to perform upon honour before the next meeting." In this way, he learned the Italian language. Subsequently he acquired sufficient knowledge of Spanish to enable him to read books in that tongue. He studied Latin a year in Boston, before he was ten years old, but since that time he had neglected it. His acquaintance now with other languages revived his taste for the Latin, however, so that he mastered that.

Surely here is literary work enough for a youth who is earning a livelihood by hard labour, having only snatches of time to devote to reading and study. There is no work of his whole life that is more replete with interest than this; for it shows that he possessed indomitable energy and force of character, together with other valuable traits. He proved that it was possible for him to be a scholar while he was a printer.

The "Junto" appears to have been copied in England, half a century after this period. When the celebrated Canning was in his youth, being educated at Oxford, a debating society was organized, limited to the number of six, who met every Thursday evening at the rooms of the members. At each meeting, before they separated, the subject for the next meeting was voted and recorded. Here Canning and Jenkinson (who became Earl of

Liverpool) made their first speeches, and here they received impulses that helped them on to fame.

Franklin began to think more of religion, and to raise some queries respecting his former doubts, soon after he came back from England. The two young men whose religious sentiments he corrupted and unsettled turned out badly, and cheated him out of a sum of money, and this led him to inquire if it was not because they ignored religious principle. He witnessed other conduct among those who talked lightly of religion, which caused him to inquire, whether, after all, his parents were not in the right. He stayed away from meeting, and devoted the Sabbath to study, which had a very bad look. Yet, he said, "I never was without some religious principle. I never doubted the existence of a Deity; that He made the world and governed it by his providence; that the most acceptable service of God was the doing good to man; that our souls are immortal; and that all crimes will be punished, and virtue rewarded, either here or hereafter." He also subscribed something for the support of the only Presbyterian meeting in Philadelphia, and advocated the importance of sustaining public worship.

The minister called upon him, and counselled him to attend church, just when he was beginning to think better of it, and it had the effect to bring him out occasionally. Once he went five Sabbaths in succession. But the preacher was dull and uninteresting, so that Franklin was not well pleased; still he continued to attend occasionally, until, one Sabbath, the preacher took the following text: "Finally, brethren, whatsoever things are true, honest, just, pure, lovely, or of good report, if there be any virtue, or any praise, think on these things." The minister was usually doctrinal in his style of preaching, but now Franklin thought he would have something practical. Consequently he was sadly disappointed when he found that the discourse embraced only the following points:—1. Keeping holy the Sabbath-day. 2. Being diligent in reading the Scriptures. 3. Attending duly public worship. 4. Partaking of the Sacrament. 5. Paying a due respect to God's ministers. Franklin thought that these subjects, though very good, did not belong to such a text, and he was so dissatisfied with the sermon, that he ceased attending.

Conscience, however, did not slumber. He saw and felt that he was wrong, and, in order to make himself better, he began to lead a self-righteous life. He imposed religious duties upon himself. He returned to the use of a form of prayer which he prepared some time before, when his thoughts were dwelling upon religious things. In that prayer, under the head of "Thanks," occurs the following:—

> "For the common benefits of air and light, for useful fire and delicious water,—Good God, I thank Thee!

"For knowledge and literature, and every useful art; for my friends and their prosperity, and for the fewness of my enemies,—Good God, I thank Thee!

"For all thy innumerable benefits; for life, and reason, and the use of speech; for health, and joy, and every pleasant hour,—My good God, I thank Thee!"

He made a little book, in which he wrote down certain virtues that he ought to cultivate, and prepared a table for the same. The following were the virtues:—

"1. Temperance.—Eat not to dulness; drink not to elevation.

"2. Silence.—Speak not but what may benefit others or yourself; avoid trifling conversation.

"3. Order.—Let all your things have their places; let each part of your business have its time.

"4. Resolution.—Resolve to perform what you ought; perform without fail what you resolve.

"5. Frugality.—Make no expense but to do good to others or yourself; that is, waste nothing.

"6. Industry.—Lose no time; be always employed in something useful; cut off all unnecessary actions.

"7. Sincerity.—Use no hurtful deceit; think innocently and justly; and, if you speak, speak accordingly.

"8. Justice.—Wrong none by doing injuries, or omitting the benefits that are your duty.

"9. Moderation.—Avoid extremes; forbear resenting injuries so much as you think they deserve.

"10. Cleanliness.—Tolerate no uncleanliness in body, clothes, or habitation.

"11. Tranquillity.—Be not disturbed at trifles, or at accidents, common or unavoidable.

"12. Chastity.

"13. Humility.—Imitate Jesus Christ and Socrates."

These are very good so far as they go, and they show that he studied to form a high character, although he had not yet attained to the height of the true Christian.

CHAPTER XXV.

CONCLUSION.

WE have followed the subject of this volume from the time he paid *too dear for his whistle*, to the period when he was well established in business. We have seen what his character was as a PRINTER-BOY, and hence his promise of success. He was not perfect by any means; on the other hand, he had marked failings. Yet, underneath the whole, we have discovered certain qualities that are indispensable to eminence in one's vocation. And now it remains to see, briefly, whether the principle we advocate was true in his case, namely, "that the boy is father of the man." To do this, we shall pass over a series of years, and take a succinct view of his position and influence in middle and advanced life.

It should be recorded first, however, that the difficulty between himself and his brother James was adjusted, ten years after his first visit to Boston. James had removed and settled in Newport, where he was fast declining in health, and Benjamin went thither to see him. Their past differences were forgotten, and their interview was signalized by mutual forgiveness. It was then that Benjamin promised to take his brother's little son, ten years old, after the father was no more, and bring him up to the printing business. This pledge he fulfilled, doing even more for the lad than he promised, for he sent him to school two or three years before he took him into the office, and finally he established him in business. This, certainly, was a happy termination of a quarrel that was creditable to neither party. The result was decisive evidence that both parties deplored their conduct towards each other.

While he was yet a young man, he was promoted to different posts of distinction. He filled various offices in Philadelphia, and served the State of Pennsylvania in several public ways, in all of which he did himself honour. He devoted a portion of his time to philosophical studies, in which he earned a world-wide fame. His mind was ever busy in projects to benefit society, and no work was too humble for him to do for the good of others. At one time he is found inventing a stove for domestic use, called afterward the Franklin stove, with which Governor Thomas was so well pleased, that he offered him a patent for the sole vending of them for a series of years; but Franklin refused it, on the ground, "*that, as we enjoy great advantages from the invention of others, we should be glad of an opportunity to serve others by any invention of ours; and this we should do freely and generously.*" This was another instance of his remarkable generosity, and it reminds us of that incident of his life in France, when an English clergyman asked him for pecuniary assistance. He gave him liberally, remarking, "Some time or other you may have an opportunity of assisting with an equal sum a stranger who has equal need of it. Do so. By that means you may discharge any obligation you may suppose yourself under to me. *Enjoin him to do the same on occasion.* By pursuing such a practice, much good may be done with little money. Let kind offices go round. Mankind are all of a family."

At another time he is engaged in improving the lamps that light the city, and devising ways of cleaning the streets. Then, again, he is originating a system of volunteer militia for the defence of his country. Extinguishing fires, also, is a subject that commands his thoughts, and he organized the first fire company in the land. Again, the education of youth demands his time, and he labours to introduce a system of schools, and finally founds a University. Thus the humblest acts of a good citizen were performed in connection with the nobler deeds of the philosopher and statesman.

The following is a brief synopsis of the offices he filled, and the honours he won:—

> HE WAS LEGISLATOR FOR PENNSYLVANIA IN 1732, WHEN ONLY TWENTY-SIX YEARS OF AGE.
>
> HE FOUNDED THE UNIVERSITY OF PENNSYLVANIA.
>
> DEPUTY POSTMASTER-GENERAL IN 1752.
>
> INVENTOR OF LIGHTNING-RODS.
>
> WAS ELECTED A FELLOW OF THE ROYAL SOCIETY.
>
> ORIGINATOR OF THE VOLUNTEER MILITIA.
>
> COLONEL OF MILITIA.
>
> MINISTER TO THE COURT OF ENGLAND IN 1764.
>
> MEMBER OF THE CONTINENTAL CONGRESS IN 1775.
>
> MINISTER PLENIPOTENTIARY TO FRANCE IN 1776.
>
> CONCLUDED FIRST TREATY FOR AMERICA IN 1778.
>
> RECEIVED THE DEGREE OF LL.D. FROM OXFORD UNIVERSITY.
>
> MINISTER PLENIPOTENTIARY TO FRANCE IN 1778.
>
> ONE OF FIVE TO DRAFT THE DECLARATION OF INDEPENDENCE.

Helped to frame the Constitution of the United States.

A Leader in the American Revolution.

Called the "Nestor of America" by the National Assembly of France.

Admitted to the highest Literary Assemblies of Europe.

Like Washington, "first in war, first in peace, and first in the hearts of his countrymen."

Honoured as a great Philosopher, sagacious Statesman, and sincere Philanthropist.

In reading the history of the United States, no name is more conspicuous than that of Franklin. His agency is everywhere seen and acknowledged in laying the foundation of her institutions, and achieving her glories. The memory of no patriot and philosopher has been more dear to generations that have come and gone since his day. Abroad, as well as at home, he was honoured. At one time, in France, "prints, medallion portraits, and busts of Franklin were multiplied throughout France; and rings, bracelets, canes, and snuff-boxes, bearing his likeness, were worn or carried quite generally." In England, and other parts of Europe, similar homage was paid to his greatness. Since that period his statue has been erected in the halls of learning and legislation, literary societies have adopted his name to give them pre-eminence, and numerous towns have been called after him. The author's native place was named in honour of Franklin, who afterwards presented the town with a valuable library that is still in existence. On being informed by a friend that this town had adopted his name, he inquired what sort of a present would be acceptable to the inhabitants as an acknowledgment of their respect and homage. The friend suggested that a *bell* might prove a timely gift, as they were erecting a new house of worship. But Franklin thought otherwise, and decided to present a library. He jocosely remarked, in the letter which accompanied the books, that he "*supposed a town that would adopt his name must be more fond of sense than sound.*"

It would multiply the pages of this volume beyond its designed limits to enumerate all the public posts of honour that Franklin adorned, and all the marks of respect that have been paid to his memory. This brief reference to the more prominent of these is sufficient to afford the reader a view of the REMARKABLE MAN, and to illustrate the force of energy, industry, integrity, and perseverance, in human destiny.

Washington wrote to him: "If to be venerated for benevolence, if to be admired for talents, if to be esteemed for patriotism, if to be beloved for philanthropy, can gratify the human mind, you must have the pleasing consolation to know that you have not lived in vain. And I flatter myself that it will not be ranked among the least grateful occurrences of your life to be assured that, so long as I retain my memory, you will be recollected with respect, veneration, and affection, by your sincere friend, George Washington."

Congress was in session when Franklin died, and when his death was announced, on motion of Madison, it was resolved that a badge of mourning be worn for one month, "as a mark of veneration due to the memory of a citizen whose native genius was not more an ornament to human nature than his various exertions of it have been precious to science, to freedom, and to his country."

In France, Condorcet eulogized him in the Academy of Science, and Mirabeau in the National Assembly. The latter said: "Antiquity would have erected altars to this great and powerful genius."

When Rachel was dying, she named her infant son "Ben-oni," which means, "son of my sorrow," because he was the occasion of her sufferings and death. But Jacob, his father, called him "Benjamin," which signifies "the son of a right hand." There was a time when Franklin's mother, weeping over her runaway boy, would have called him "Ben-oni," and it might have appeared to observers that he would turn out to be such. But the excellent lessons of his early home, and the good traits of character which he nurtured, caused him to become a true Benjamin to his parents,—"a son of their right hand." With a warm, filial heart, he sought to minister to their wants in their declining years, and, as we have seen, offered the last and highest tribute of affection in his power, when they were laid in the dust.

In his riper years, Franklin sincerely regretted the doubts of his youth and early manhood respecting religion. The sentiments that were poured into his young mind by fond, parental lips, he came to respect and cherish. He went to the house of God on the Sabbath with great constancy; and, if recollecting the sin of his youth, he wrote to his daughter, "*Go constantly to church, whoever preaches.*" His own experience taught him that it was dangerous and wicked to forsake the sanctuary. He became interested in every good work. His influence and his purse were offered to sustain Christianity. He appreciated every benevolent enterprise, and bade them God-speed. On one occasion the celebrated Whitefield preached in behalf of an orphan asylum, which he proposed to erect in Georgia. Franklin was not in full sympathy with the plan, because he thought it should be erected in Pennsylvania, and the orphans brought there. Still, he listened to the eminent preacher unprejudiced, and when the collection was taken, at the close of the meeting, he emptied his pockets of all the money he had, which consisted of "a handful of copper money, three or four silver dollars, and five pistoles in gold."

He sympathized deeply with the poor and needy, and espoused the cause of the oppressed in every land. He was the first President of the Pennsylvania Anti-Slavery Society, and both his hand and heart were pledged to the cause of freedom. One of his biographers, summing up his character in these particulars, says: "He was bold, consistent, active, and greatly in advance of his age. From his Quaker brethren in Philadelphia he contracted all their zeal in behalf of humanity, although in his mind it put on the aspect of plain, practical beneficence. He was ever foremost in all humane enterprises. He was never misled, through sympathy with a majority, into the support of measures which, though popular, were inconsistent with a high-toned Christian morality. He was the champion of the Indians when to advocate their cause was to displease many. He was one of the earliest opponents of the slave-trade and slavery. He omitted no opportunity to protest against war and its iniquity, and he branded as piracy the custom of privateering, however sanctioned by international usages. As a statesman and philosopher his name is imperishable. As an active benefactor of his race, he is entitled to its lasting gratitude. As one of the founders of the American Union, he must ever be held in honourable remembrance by all who prize American institutions. As the zealous foe to oppression in all its forms, he merits the thankful regard of good men of all ages and climes."

He carried his reverence for God and his regard for Christianity into the high places of authority. He proposed the first Day of Fasting and Prayer ever observed in Pennsylvania, and wrote the proclamation for the Secretary of State. When the convention to frame the Constitution of the United States met in Philadelphia, in 1787, he introduced a motion into that body for daily prayers, which, strange to say, was rejected. In support of his motion, he made the following memorable address, which fairly illustrates his usual disposition to recognize God in all human affairs:—

> "In the beginning of the contest with Britain, when we were sensible of danger, we had daily prayers in this room for Divine protection. Our prayers, sir, were heard; and they were graciously answered. All of us, who were engaged in the struggle, must have observed frequent instances of a superintending Providence in our favour. To that kind Providence we owe this happy opportunity of consulting in peace on the means of establishing our future national felicity. And have we now forgotten that

powerful Friend, or do we imagine we no longer need his assistance? I have lived, sir, a long time; and the longer I live, the more convincing proofs I see of this truth, *that God governs in the affairs of men.* And, if a sparrow cannot fall to the ground without his notice, is it probable that an empire can arise without his aid? We have been assured, sir, in the sacred writings, that, 'except the Lord build the house, they labour in vain that build it.' I firmly believe this; and I also believe, that, without his concurring aid, we shall succeed in this political building no better than the builders of Babel; we shall be divided by our little, partial, local interests; our projects will be confounded, and we ourselves shall become a reproach and a by-word down to future ages. And, what is worse, mankind may hereafter, from this unfortunate instance, despair of establishing government by human wisdom, and leave it to chance, war, and conquest. I therefore beg leave to move, that henceforth prayers, imploring the assistance of Heaven, and its blessing on our deliberations, be held in this assembly every morning before we proceed to business; and that one or more of the clergy of this city be requested to officiate in that service."

His confidence in the Christian religion, and his regard for purity of conduct, did not diminish as he drew near the grave. On the other hand, he bore earnest testimony to the faith of his fathers until the close of his life, and, ere he died, renewed his vindication of the Scriptures, in the following circumstances.

A young man called to see him, as he lay upon his death-bed, scarcely able to articulate. Dr. Franklin welcomed him with a benignant look, which he was wont to cast upon the young, and imparted some good advice to him.

"What is your opinion with regard to the truth of the Scriptures?" inquired the young man, who was somewhat sceptical.

Franklin replied, although in a very feeble state, "Young man, my advice to you is, that you cultivate an acquaintance with, and a firm belief in, the Holy Scriptures; this is your certain interest."

THE END.

Milton Keynes UK
Ingram Content Group UK Ltd.
UKHW030624061024
449204UK00004B/329